A BOY'S HOLOCAUST

By Dr. Lewis Reznik

Best wishes

© 2010 Dr. Lewis Reznik
All Rights Reserved.
Cover Illustration © 2010 Daniel Lieff Revkin

No part of this publication may be reproduced, stored in a retrieval system, or transmitted, in any form or by any means, electronic, mechanical, photocopying, recording, or otherwise, without the written permission of the author.

First published by Dog Ear Publishing
4010 W. 86th Street, Ste H
Indianapolis, IN 46268
www.dogearpublishing.net

dog ear
PUBLISHING

ISBN: 978-160844-634-6
Library of Congress Control Number: 2010931304

This book is printed on acid-free paper.

Printed in the United States of America

Praise for *A Boy's Holocaust*

"I consider this type of literature to be essential to the understanding of the Holocaust and its manifold implications."

— Prof. Elie Wiesel,
winner of the Nobel Peace Prize,
author of "Night"

"This is a powerful book written by a man who miraculously survived the Holocaust. Reading the personal details has an impact you may not expect. No histrionics - just emotionally loaded facts. I know Dr. Lew Reznik and his eyes silently confirm the contents. I strongly suggest you read *A Boy's Holocaust*."

— Steve Reich,
winner of the 2009 Pulitzer Prize
for musical composition

"Powerfully portrays the unrelenting threats faced by those struggling to survive in those awful times..."

— Paul Slovic,
Prof. of Psychology, Univ. of Oregon,
leading authority on genocide

For my beloved daughter, Michelle,
whose life was tragically cut short

Foreword

My memories do not allow me to abandon my past, even though I have repressed them for more than half a century. A happy early childhood was transformed into a horrific period, and within a few years, I became a part of what history now calls the Holocaust. Surviving this dark era makes it possible for me to appreciate any joy or success life brings, no matter how infinitesimal or fleeting. Luck was on my side, but peace of mind continues to elude me. For those interested in knowing about the events and hardships that befell the Jews and me on the Eastern Front during World War II, this is my story.

This memoir has grown out of a request made in the spring of 1987 by my daughter, Michelle, of blessed memory. At that time, she was elected President of the Jewish Association at Williams College. It was her task to organize a *Yom Hashoah* (Holocaust Remembrance Day) program. She approached me and asked whether I would like to be the speaker at the service and describe my experiences during the Holocaust. It was through her urging that I reached back to those terrible years. I dedicate this account to her and to the memory of my brother Aron, of blessed memory, who gave so much of himself by protecting me from what would have been a horrendous death. I would also like to express my gratitude and appreciation to my beloved wife, Louise, and my dear daughter, Donna, for their invaluable assistance and patience in editing my manuscript. Without their support this story would never be published. My appreciation also goes to Andrew Revkin for taking on responsibility for editing and publishing my manuscript, and to his son, Daniel Revkin, who created the drawing for the book cover.

CHAPTER 1

Before the War

I was born on or around August 20, 1930, in a small town called Janów Polaski, near the city of Pinsk in eastern Poland. It was the custom not to register dates of birth since birthdays were not considered important. I was the youngest of five children. My brother Aron was the oldest, and three sisters followed him — Malka, Chaya (known as Helen), and Leah (called Liza). Five thousand people lived in our town, half of them Gentiles and half of them Jews. Most of the Jews were craftsmen or shopkeepers who could barely make a living, but they were less poor than the local Christian peasants. By the town's standards, my family was considered well off. My town can best be described as a *shtetl* (a small town in Eastern Europe).

I believe that there was only one two-story structure. No home had indoor plumbing, and water had to be brought in from a common pump. Few of the homes had electricity. Some of the roofs were covered with thatch, and it was not uncommon to see stork nests atop the houses. There were two main intersecting streets and very few side streets. The town was located in the Pripet Marshes, and when the snow melted, the streets turned into impassable rivers of mud. An outdoor market was located in the center of town. The winters were extremely severe. To keep warm, the women who sold merchandise would keep a pot of smoldering coal between their legs under their long coats. At times, the coal would singe their coats. Obviously, it was quite a sight. In Janów, we owned our house, which was made of brick, and my paternal grandmother's house was located in the same courtyard as ours. Though there were hardships, our family life was rather pleasant.

World War II began on September 1, 1939. The years preceding the war did not seem particularly dangerous to me, although growing up as a Jew in a Polish town did pose disadvantages. Anti-Semitism was a fact of life even before the war. As children, we encountered verbal threats and occasional physical abuse from the Gentile boys. However, we never experienced pogroms (spontaneous or organized riots that were frequently perpetrated in Russia against the Jews, resulting in injury, death and property destruction).

Anti-Jewish feelings ran extremely high during Christmas and especially around Easter, because of their association with the birth and crucifixion of Christ. Even some of the Catholic priests espoused virulent anti-Semitism and contributed to the hatred. On those holidays, Jews were reluctant to venture outside their homes for fear of being assaulted. In our area, many peasants still clung to the old belief that Christian blood was used in the baking of matzos. It was not uncommon for Jews to be beaten and Jewish homes vandalized. I still recall the sense of uneasiness sitting at home and listening to the commotion and rowdiness in the street. I must indicate that not every Jew was timid. One Jewish boy in particular, Judel Reznik (no relation), was considered a *shtarker* (tough guy). He would always hold his ground and challenge those hooligans.

During my preschool years, we had two homes. One was on an estate in the forest of Zawishcze, near Janów. Our house in Zawishcze was fairly spacious. My family lived in one wing, and the families of two long-term employees lived in the adjacent wing. The wooden structure was located near a lake surrounded by acres and acres of woods. Bordering the house was a stable where we kept our horses and cows and stored hay during the winter. In Zawishcze, my father owned a turpentine distillery that also produced charcoal and tar. In addition, he manufactured cement roof shingles and pipes for water wells, and supplied firewood to the inhabitants of Janów. My brother, Aron, dropped out of school to become my father's assistant, although my father was not pleased with Aron's decision.

My father, Pinchas, of blessed memory, was generally respected and admired by his peers and workers and was adored by his family. In my opinion, my dad was a *lamed vovnik* – a righteous and pious man. My father never took advantage of his employees and treated them fairly and kindly, and extended credit to them to purchase flour and other necessities. The unique relationship my father developed with his employees made us confident that we could depend on their support if and when the need arose. In essence, I am alive today partly due to the esteem and loyalty my father received from his employees.

My paternal grandfather, Simcha, died when my father was still a little boy, and my grandmother Ethel, of blessed memory, didn't have the financial means to support her four children. As a small child, my father attended a *yeshiva* (a Jewish religious school for boys). Some of the rabbis who taught at this school were notorious for their brutal treatment of students. It seemed that those pupils whose families paid full tuition were spared punishment, while the poorer ones would bear the brunt of the rabbis' frustration. Since my father was the poorest of the poor, he frequently was the recipient of the teachers' wrath. Because my grandmother was unable to provide my father with daily meals, he was a *kest kind*, a person receiving charitable meals from the community. Jewish families in town fed him on a rotational basis. Helping orphans was considered to be a *mitzvah* — an obligation to perform a good deed amongst the Jews. Despite all his deprivations, my father grew up to be a prominent citizen in our community.

Grandmother Ethel was a stern, skinny, proud woman with dark, penetrating eyes, who rarely showed her emotions. She was extremely partial to her daughter, my father's sister Bashka, and Bashka's daughter, Malka. During my school years, Grandma Ethel often took the role of mother to me when she stayed in Janów. When Grandma Ethel grew old and her hands became arthritic to the point that she could no longer perform all of her household chores, she would often ask me to help her. I remember washing the floors, and if I inadvertently missed a spot, she would crossly point out my error and say, *"Leibele ot-to-do"* — "Lewis, over here and there," commanding me to go over the missed spaces again. Even though she was demanding, we showed Grandma Ethel great respect because we loved our father so much. Although my maternal grandmother, Feigl, of blessed memory, passed away when I was very young, I remember her as a much more affectionate person. She lived with my mother's brother, Dovid Warshawski.

The practice of giving *tzedakah* (charity or charitable deeds) was always stressed in our home, as it was throughout our community. Years later, each Friday before the Jewish Sabbath, indigent people would come to my Grandma Ethel's house for a weekly contribution, and she would always have something set aside for them. The fundamental principle of charity was instilled in all of us. The *pushke* (a blue and white box for collecting monetary contributions for charitable deeds) was always present in Jewish homes, schools, and synagogues. I recall bringing lunches or providing lunch money to a poor boy in my class. But of all the unfortunate people, a woman named Malka Lash stands out most prominently in my memory. Her sole source of support came from her benefactors. She had a peculiar hiccup that was audible a block away when she walked through our town. Malka Lash was also a fixture at Jewish funeral processions, where she was sure to escort the deceased and proclaim to the mourners, "charity will sustain the living."

My mother, Bella (Beylke), of blessed memory, was a true *yiddishe mame*, a kind and sympathetic Jewish mother. She was both beautiful and devoted to us. My family treated Mother like a princess. She was a frail woman, whom my father adored and placed on a pedestal, and we continued to keep her there throughout her life. For a woman who was raised at the beginning of the twentieth century in Janów, my mother was well educated. She could speak fluent Hebrew, Russian, Polish, and Yiddish. She had even studied the Bible as a child, an unusual accomplishment in those years, since most Jewish women were denied that level of education. Later in life, she frequently questioned and disagreed with passages written in the Scriptures. Because of our reverence for her and her frailty, my mother became totally dependent upon us when we later settled in America, and she had no social life outside her home. Despite her seclusion, she remained well informed throughout her life, and read the *Jewish Forward* newspaper in Yiddish until the day she died. Mother was the lynchpin that held our family together from the day we escaped from the Nazis, in the fall of 1942, until her death in 1982 at the age of 94.

When we were small children in Zawishcze, my parents hired a tutor to live with us. But as each of us grew older, we were sent away to a school in Janów, while my parents remained in Zawishcze, the family place of business. This meant that my sister Liza and I had to board at different homes in Janów, sometimes with strangers. She and I were the first in our family to attend a Hebrew Day School. My older siblings went to public school, and received instruction in the Hebrew language and religion after school. One year, my sister Liza and I boarded with a woman named Itta. I was not the ideal boarder, and often rebelled because I was away from my parents. Itta was justifiably annoyed with my behavior, but she needed the extra income and had to put up with my nonsense. I was a very picky eater and, at times, would demand a meal that was neither cooked, nor baked, nor fried. Other times, I would ask for foods that were impossible for her to cook. Religious Jews will not work on the Sabbath, and cooking is prohibited. One Saturday afternoon I demanded a fried egg. There was no way Itta could have profaned the Sabbath by lighting a fire to fry the egg, but that fact did not deter me from being obnoxious and demanding my meal. I still remember screaming incessantly, *"Itta, a preznbitze! Itta a preznbitze!"* "Itta, a scrambled egg! Itta, a scrambled egg!" Itta just sat there, seething with anger, but she didn't utter a word in response.

Because I did not have my parents around, it was easy for me to neglect my studies and get in trouble with the teachers. Often a teacher would call my parents for a conference to discuss my lagging scholastic progress. Most of the time my father would show up for these occasions. The conferences would usually be held in the classroom, in front of all my classmates, who were of course eager to see my father dish out his punishment right there on the spot. But instead, my father would address me with great affection, gently exhorting me to reform by affectionately saying, "*Leibele*, you will improve." Inevitably he would take out some coins and give them to me as an incentive. Those acts of kindness have always remained in my mind and in my heart, and to this day I cherish the memories of his respect and love for me.

After finishing Polish public school, my eldest sister, Malka, furthered her education in the town of Kovel, while my other sister, Helen, attended the Hebrew Gymnasium (high school) in Pinsk. Our family was reunited in Zawishcze only during school breaks. Those were very special times in a special place, and we all loved them, for the whole family was together and my parents were around every day.

The forests of Zawishcze were a child's dream world, too. We had cows, chickens, dogs, and horses, and access to a lake for boating, fishing, and skating during the winter. Seemingly unlimited fields and forests gave us places to roam and play. We grew our own food and processed our own dairy products. Going home during the winter break was an experience in itself. The winters were extremely cold and the snow would stay on the ground from early November until April. I was bundled up in sheepskin to keep out the cold. Sheep hair invariably wound up in my mouth, and the memory of the odor of the hide still permeates my nostrils. The distance home from my school in Janów was no more than 12 miles, but it took several hours to complete the journey by horse and sleigh. At home, we didn't have many other children of our age to play with, but my brother and sisters and I enjoyed walking together on the frozen lake, sledding down hills, skating on the ice, and going on sleigh rides with the whole family. There was something especially enjoyable about riding in the forest in complete serenity, with the silence broken only by the sound of sleigh bells.

The forest and its surrounding land belonged to a Polish noble named Graff Poslawski. He had a passion for hunting, and during the winter season he invited many of his friends to participate in the sport. After a snowfall, in anticipation of a successful hunt, he would close traffic in the forest to all but those who were in the hunting party. Many villagers were engaged in flushing out the animals by creating noises and directing the prey toward the hunters. Although we were not involved in the hunt, it was exciting to watch the preparations.

The Jewish holy season takes place in September and October. On the two major holidays, Rosh Hashanah (the Jewish New Year) and Yom Kippur (the Day of Atonement that follows ten days after Rosh Hashanah), Jews come to synagogue to pray, welcome in the New Year, and ask for forgiveness for past transgressions. These special days are called the High Holidays, and to celebrate them, my family traveled to and stayed over in Janów to attend religious services in the synagogue. On those holy days, my father was accorded the honor of conducting the *Mussaf* Service, part of the service and prayers during the Sabbath and on other special holidays. He did this with great feeling, emotion, and expertise. Even now, I can vividly see him standing tall before the pulpit.

Another feature of my Jewish childhood was our attachment to Palestine. Israel had not yet been founded as a modern state (this did not take place until 1948, after

World War II), but Jews had longed for their biblical homeland over the centuries. Like many others, my family was staunch Zionists. Zionism is a political movement that strives for the return of the Jews from Diaspora to Palestine. Before the war I belonged to the Zionist youth movement, *Hashomer Hatzair*, a group somewhat structured like the Boy Scouts. As a child, I fantasized about living in what was then called Palestine, but since my father was a prosperous businessman, emigration was not a logical option. Our standard of living was better than what we would experience in Palestine. Nevertheless, my sisters made a commitment to speak only Hebrew amongst themselves and with my parents, and I sometimes think that if we were poorer and had immigrated to Palestine, we would have been spared the horrors of World War II.

Our dreams, however, were suddenly put on hold. Throughout the summer of 1939, there was anticipation and fear of impending war. Even so, that summer my father prepared to renovate his turpentine distillery. As a result, his workers concluded (or rationalized) that since Dad was refurbishing the turpentine distillery, war was not imminent. This was a further indication of the confidence and respect the workers had for him. But the tragic events that were to follow were beyond his control.

CHAPTER 2

War

In September 1939, Poland was partitioned between Nazi Germany and Soviet Russia, and our town was placed under Soviet occupation. I will never forget the tragic events of September 1, 1939, the day the Germans invaded Poland. It was a Friday afternoon, and as my mother was preparing for the Sabbath, we turned on the radio and heard the newscaster announce the German invasion. The radio announcer vowed that the attack would be repulsed, and that the invaders would be driven off Polish soil. "Poland will be victorious in the end!" he assured his listeners. My mother started pulling her hair. At that time, I couldn't comprehend the gravity of the situation and why it was affecting her that way. Now I know that she remembered the hardships her family had endured during World War I and was, therefore, more cognizant of the implications of this calamity. Within a week of the outbreak of hostilities, it was obvious that Poland had lost the war. We had to abandon our delusion that following England and France's entry into the conflict, Germany would be contained. Despite my mother's concern and distress, there was no way that she, or for that matter anyone, could have anticipated the full horror of the dreadful events to be unleashed in Poland, and on the Jewish people in particular.

The NSDAP, The National Socialist German Worker Party (Nazis), had a longstanding policy of hatred against the Jews. In their party platform of February 24, 1920, it was stated that a Jew could never be considered a German, and therefore, could never be a German citizen. When the Nazis came to power in 1935, they instituted the Nuremberg Laws, a series of inhumane measures against the German Jewish population. The aim of those decrees was to put pressure on Jews to leave Germany, and then seize their property once they were gone. To accomplish their goal, a series of drastic measures were undertaken. Jews were expelled from all civil service and government positions. The universities were forced to expel all Jewish professors and then later on all Jewish students. Jewish children in public schools were ridiculed and taunted. Jewish physicians were barred from government hospitals. All marital union between Germans and Jews was forbidden. Jewish shops were boycotted.

The Nazi-controlled press kept up a relentless hate campaign against the German Jews that led to the infamous *Kristallnacht* (Crystal Night) pogrom of November 9 and 10, 1938. During those two days and nights, all Jewish synagogues were burned to the ground. Many Jewish businesses had their windows broken. Homes were looted, several Jews were killed, and many Jewish men were incarcerated in a concentration camp. Those events had all been described in the papers and on the radio, and we were aware of them as we anticipated the arrival of the German armies any day.

Fortunately, in accordance with provisions of the Russo-German Treaty of August 1939, our town came under Russian occupation, and we were spared the German occupation, at least for a little while. The noblemen from our town of Zawishcze fled to Romania and then to Italy. Streams of refugees, mostly Jews who were running from the advancing German invaders, arrived in our region. These refugees brought stories of German mistreatment, but we dismissed most of their talk as propaganda, or at best as ploys to elicit sympathy from us because they lost their homes. No one could comprehend, or was willing to believe, their accounts. It seemed preposterous that a civilized nation like Germany was capable of committing such barbarism.

For the moment, Germany was not an issue — but Russia was. At first, I was unable to understand the meaning of the political and socio-economic changes that my family faced as a result of the Russian occupation. I was just a child, and was very happy that the opening of school was delayed. In addition, since the Communist slogans proclaimed equality for all, it seemed as though the advantages for the Jews were obvious. Soon I was indoctrinated into the Communist youth movement. I considered it an extreme honor to be initiated into the Young Pioneers (Communist Boy Scouts with political overtones). I was issued a red bandana and tie ring, and was made the drummer of the unit.

Though I was a youngster, I had mixed feelings about the Soviet regime. Many young men in our town also knew the true nature of Communism and decided to cross the border illegally into Lithuania, and from there immigrate to Japan. They eventually wound up in China. Anti-Semitism, which had been supported by the state under the Polish regime, was abolished under Communism, and there were no overt signs of hatred toward Jews. Most students who previously attended the Hebrew Day School now enrolled in the Russian Jewish Day School. But at our first assembly, before the new school year began, Principal Marmor addressed us in Hebrew for the last time. The Hebrew language was suddenly considered subversive and was banned. It was odd to hear him speak in Yiddish right after the assembly ended.

Yiddish became the accepted language and was taught as a subject, and Yiddish plays were frequently performed in our town. Hebrew was equated with Zionism, which was considered subversive. Zionism was considered nationalism, a philosophy in competition with Communism, while Yiddish was the language of an ethnic minority living in the Soviet Union. In addition, Hebrew is the language of the Bible, and religion was banned by the Communists, so the language was forbidden.

Troubles quickly mounted. Shortly after the Russian occupation, my father's business was confiscated without any compensation, and he was obligated to run the business for the state. If his production quota was not met, he was responsible for the failure — an act tantamount to sabotage, which carried severe consequences. Eventually he was released from his responsibilities and became a common laborer in Janów. Dad was significantly relieved not to have to carry the burden of such a responsibility, which could have landed him in jail.

Living under the Communist regime meant that we were constantly afraid of being deported to Siberia, a place that was a metaphor for deprivation and death. The Russians considered merchants and people of wealth to be "parasites" — an undesirable class that exploited the working masses. Since most of the Jews were small-time merchants, they were placed in that category. Most of the Gentiles who were at risk of being persecuted by the Communists fled to German-occupied Poland, in advance of the Russian arrival. The Communists expelled wealthy people from the large cities and forbade them to dwell in areas near the borders. In order to leave town, people needed to obtain travel permits. In addition, merchants' passports were stamped with a note called *Paragraph 11*, symbolizing their profession's untrustworthy status.

As previously mentioned, many Jewish refugees from western Poland arrived in our area shortly after the outbreak of World War II. In the confusion that followed, family members often became separated. In the spring of 1940, the Soviet authorities informed all refugees from western Poland that they would have to decide whether to take on Soviet citizenship or to return home to the area that was now under German occupation. Many of the refugees who settled in eastern Poland simply missed their families and wished to be reunited. Consequently they declined Soviet citizenship. According to Russian logic, since these refugees wished to return home, the Soviets suspected them of being foreign agents. One summer night, and without any forewarning, the NKVD, the arm of the law responsible for internal security that later came to be known as the KGB, entered the homes of people who had refused Soviet citizenship. It was the middle of the night, and the Communists gave them only two hours to pack. They were loaded into boxcars and exiled to Siberia. Ironically, they were the lucky ones, since most of them survived the war despite enormous hardship.

In the summer of 1940, we learned that the Nazis had overrun Belgium and the Netherlands, and that France had capitulated to them as well. War between the Soviet Union and Germany was inevitable. In anticipation, the Communist regime began building military airports and fortifications in our area, since we lived only 50 miles from the new border with Germany. Early in 1941 and continuing into the spring of that year, massive transports of male and female Russian civilian prisoners arrived in Janów. These prisoners, who had committed only minor offenses under the Russian regime — such as being late for work, missing a day of work, or trading in the black market — were forced to build military airfields and other fortifications.

The second mass deportation to Siberia took place that June. Shortly before the deportation, a large number of Russian soldiers, wearing green army caps, appeared in our town. The soldiers were part of the border guard and were under the command of the internal security organs, and we had a premonition that something terrible was about to occur. On Friday night, June 20, the soldiers entered the homes of individuals who had *Paragraph 11* stamped on their passports and they were forcibly removed. For the most part, the victims were Jewish. The soldiers, once again, informed them that they had a short time to gather their belongings. They were then taken to the railroad station and loaded onto boxcars.

On Saturday, June 21, many people turned out to bid farewell to those who were destined to be deported. As the people bemoaned the fate of the deportees, one man, Beryl Divinski, who was on the transport, made a dire prediction. He stated, "You who are left behind will envy us, the exiles." It remains a mystery to me how he could have predicted the ensuing horrors. That Saturday night, or early Sunday morning, the transport left the station. The rest of us were left with a sense of foreboding. We wondered when our turn would come.

CHAPTER 3

The Invasion

On Sunday at about noon, I heard machine-gun fire and planes flying over our town. We soon learned that Germany had invaded Russia. True disaster now began to unfold. The Russians declared martial law and ordered total mobilization, but the majority of the peasants disobeyed this order since they believed that the Germans would soon overrun their villages and save them from the Soviet oppressors. The biggest fear the peasants had was that the Russian occupiers would confiscate their land and they would have to work like indentured laborers on a collective farm. Most likely, this was the single most important reason why, at first, the peasants welcomed the Nazis. As it turned out, at the outbreak of the war the new invaders met very little resistance from the Russian forces. They were quickly able to encircle large numbers of retreating Russian soldiers and occupy vast areas of Russian territory. Within a week, we saw Russian soldiers withdrawing in disarray. Then, on the thirteenth day after the invasion began, the first German units reached our town of Janów. It was Friday, July 5, 1941.

When the Germans arrived, the Gentile townspeople flocked to greet them with flowers, bread, and water as a sign of hospitality and friendship. Even a Jewish woman was part of the greeting party, for she unwittingly believed that she could ingratiate herself with the Germans. She was not typical, though. While the Gentiles perceived the Germans as saviors from Communist oppression, most Jews were very apprehensive. I was overwhelmed when I saw the might of the German armies, especially after observing the ragged retreat of the Russian soldiers. The German army was well motorized and the soldiers appeared confident, rested, and ready for action. We felt that a Nazi victory was inevitable, and we anticipated that Russia would collapse in no time at all. That same day, we saw trucks filled with Russian prisoners-of-war being transported behind the German lines. The prisoners looked harried and were rightfully fearful of what lay ahead.

The next morning, Saturday, I witnessed my first episode of Nazi cruelty toward Jews. The *gabbai*, or sexton, of our synagogue, Moishe Dovid Visotski, an elderly and frail man, was walking to visit his daughter. Needless to say, his long beard and *Hasidic* garb made him look conspicuously Jewish. As soon as a group of German soldiers spotted him, he was surrounded and forced to shine their shoes and clean their bicycles. To further humiliate him, they cut off his beard. I remember how he was panting, deathly frightened, and how delighted the soldiers were. Later on, a direct order was issued for all beards to be shaved. Pious Jews considered this to be a day of mourning. For a while, some men stayed indoors rather than shave. They tried to wear handkerchiefs to cover their faces, but in the end, they had no choice but to comply.

For two weeks after the German occupation, large concentrations of *Wehrmacht* (regular German armed forces) passed through town. Some soldiers hinted at the hardships the Jews would face under German occupation; however, no one could conceive of the horror nor comprehend what the soldiers were trying to intimate to us. As the front advanced farther east, the first German troops moved out, to be replaced by another group of Germans who progressively demonstrated even greater hostility toward the Jews. It became clearer that we were in for rough times.

The Jews were also ordered to appoint representatives from the community to form a Jewish advisory body, known as the *Judenrat*. The chairman of this organization was Alter Divinski, who, prior to the war, had held a similar title in the Jewish community. He agreed to serve on the *Judenrat* with the stipulation that my father would serve with him. Serving in the *Judenrat* was a difficult assignment, to say the least. The members were responsible for appointing a Jewish police force to help carry out the orders and decrees issued by the Nazis. The *Judenrat* was responsible for supplying the Jewish workforce to the Nazis, providing a list of people who would be deported to labor camps, and collecting gold or other tribute demanded by the Germans. Frequently, the members of the *Judenrat* would endure corporal punishment at the whim of the Nazis. On occasion, the Jewish police were ordered to beat the defenseless members of the *Judenrat* that had appointed them. Alter Divinski received the largest share of punishment. Invariably, a Nazi would stand with his gun drawn over the Jewish policemen, making sure that punishment was severe enough.

For Jews, living under German occupation became more difficult each day. There were beatings, harassments, forced labor, restrictive orders, and the mandatory wearing of armbands for easy identification. The armband was changed to a yellow circle, to be worn on the outer garment, front and back, and then the circle was changed to a yellow, six-pointed Star of David, which had to be worn in the same manner by all Jews 10 years of age or older. The Nazis designated that symbol as a badge of humiliation.

It is difficult for me to convey how stigmatized I felt putting on that armband for the first time. This was a badge of shame, a badge of humiliation that singled me out for ridicule, punishment, and abuse. I had the feeling that all Gentile eyes were focused on me. It brought on feelings of despair, a sense of inferiority and, above all, fear of my gentile neighbors. I recall one incident when a gentile boy of my age confronted me. This boy rode up to me on his horse and hit me over the head with a stick. I just stood there and cried in pain, but could not retaliate.

As time went on, the Jewish community began to disintegrate. Each week, the decrees became more stringent. When bread rations were distributed, Jews had to stand in a separate line and were allowed to get their rations only after the Gentiles had their chance. Jews were not permitted to walk on the sidewalk, but only in the middle of road. When Jews approached an oncoming German soldier, they had to remove their caps and were not allowed to look at him. As Jews, we were stripped of all our rights and protection before the law, and no matter how severe an injustice might have been, we had no recourse.

CHAPTER 4

The Shoah Begins

Tisha B'Av, the ninth day of the eleventh month of the Jewish lunar calendar, a day of fasting that commemorates many tragedies that struck the Jewish people throughout history, came on Saturday, August 3, 1941, not long before my eleventh birthday. In accordance with *Halacha* (religious law), it was observed on Sunday, on the tenth of the month called *Av*. About three days before *Tisha B'Av*, rumors began circulating that neighboring areas were being scoured by units of the *Einsatz Komandos*, German roving killing squads, specifically trained and dedicated to killing civilians, especially Jews. We heard that they were massacring entire Jewish communities. Men, women, and children were shot and dumped into mass graves. At first the Jews dismissed this news as fabrication, because no one could fathom that brutality of such magnitude could be perpetrated against innocent, defenseless people. But then survivors of the massacres arrived in our town and the truth became evident. With the realization that this fate could befall us as well, our Jewish community felt trapped. Because the Jews were religious, they put their trust in God. We prayed and hoped that redemption would come from above. After all, it was *Tisha B'Av*, and everyone was praying and fasting that Sunday.

At dusk on Monday, August 4, 1941, an order was issued for all Jewish males to assemble in the market square. Immediately, the local police, under the supervision of a few German officers, began to round up Jewish men and escort them to the assembly place. Despite all that had transpired in our area, we still were unable to accept the idea that real harm would befall our community. Since our home was located in the center of town, we thought it would be safer to spend the night in my uncle's home, located on the outskirts. As we walked toward his house, we came across two local policemen who had been classmates of my siblings. They did show some civility toward my sisters and let us continue toward our uncle's home. The night dragged on as we sat in fear, anticipating that at any moment someone would pound on the door and take us away. As things turned out, my uncle's house was not raided.

The men who were held in detention at the market square were forced to kneel all night, and were then ordered to dance, sing, and perform other demeaning acts. They were also beaten. At dawn on Tuesday, August 5, 1941, they were inexplicably ordered to disperse and go home. Again we assumed that the worst was over. To this day, I am at a loss to explain why the men who were assembled that night were released. That same morning of August 5, my father went to work to load logs on flat cars, a task he was forced to do by the Germans. My brother remained at home, having the foresight to finish preparing a hiding place in the woodshed in our backyard. I went to visit my cousins who lived two streets away. As soon as I arrived, I noticed German soldiers on horseback. Unlike the regular *Wehrmacht*, these soldiers wore camouflage fatigues. Some of them were leading horses that had machine guns mounted on their backs. The Germans rode on the sidewalk, peering through the windows into the houses to observe who was inside. I had an ominous feeling and ran home.

As I rushed on, a Gentile girl, aged 16 or 17, whose last name was Horupa, urged me to take off my Jewish armband to avoid being recognized by the Germans. Before I entered my house, I alerted my brother about what I had seen, and helped him camouflage the entrance to his hiding place. While still in the woodshed, I heard the Germans enter our yard. To avoid attracting the Nazi's suspicions, I grabbed a handful of logs and pretended to be carrying in wood for cooking. A soldier came into the house and asked, *"Wo sind die Männer?"* ("Where are the men?") I froze and did not tell him anything. I still shudder and get a numb feeling when I reflect on how close my brother had come to being discovered. When the Nazis rode by a Jewish home and spotted a Jewish man through a window, they would generally dismount and seize him. No doubt, some of our Gentile neighbors were only too willing to point out the Jewish homes to the Nazis. There were countless stories of many Jews being betrayed to the butchers on that day.

In a matter of minutes, the Germans started rounding up the Jewish men of the town and herded them like cattle to the market square. The victims were forced to run while the Nazis rode behind them on horseback. I saw Jews who, having been apprehended during their morning prayers, were still wrapped in their *tallesim* (prayer shawls) as they were hurled into the assembly place. No words can describe my feelings or express the dread and anxiety I felt during that ordeal. How could one prepare for such a day? Although the roundup lasted less than three hours, it felt like an eternity. Throughout the episode, my sisters, my mother and I sat in our house in total silence. Intermittently, a member of the SS (*Shutzstaffel*, the protective "squadron special" trained and dedicated to unconditionally obey Hitler's orders, especially when it came to killing people) came into the house, peered into our rooms, and demanded to know where the men were.

When I had the courage to look out the window into the street, I saw Jewish men being forced to run to the assembly area. One man was dragged out of the neighboring house. I also saw an elderly man who was picked out of an outhouse, right behind the hideout where my brother had placed himself. Because of his age, the man moved slowly. A German kept shoving the point of his rifle into the stately, elderly gentleman, shouting "*Schnell, schnell!*" ("Faster, faster!")

We maintained hope that my father and our other male relatives were safe, since they had left for work that morning and thus might have been able to escape the roundup. As we later learned, the police had barred my father's exit from the town and he returned to my uncle's home, where he, along with our other relatives, hid in the cellar. Unfortunately, they were discovered and taken away. My sister, Liza, had a classmate who lived next door to us in the corner house. This classmate informed her that she had seen my father, along with my relatives and other Jews, being led by the SS to the marketplace. She told my sister that after my father turned the corner into our street, he kept looking back. I can only assume he was hoping to catch a glimpse of his family before he was shot to death. Within three or four hours, more than four hundred Jewish adult males were rounded up and brutalized before the eyes of their loved ones. One woman clung to her husband as an SS-man tried to take him away. When she persisted, she and her husband were shot on the spot in front of their children.

At the end of the *Aktion* (a euphemism the Nazis used for the mass roundup and execution of innocent people), the remaining victims were divided into three groups according to their level of physical fitness. They were then lined up in three columns and marched out of town. From a distance, I was able to see the columns being led away, and felt relieved because I believed that the ordeal was over. Of course, at the time I was unaware that my father was among the victims. All along the route, the men were beaten. Hooves of the horses trampled over those who fell from the blows or from exhaustion.

Then the killing began. Some were executed on the spot. The rest were marched toward the outskirts of town. Shortly after, we heard the rifle fire that marked the beginning of the destruction of our Jewish community. The elderly and sick were murdered outside the city limits near the old Jewish cemetery, and the rest were executed about two miles from the town limits in the fields of Borovicze. Only one man, Faivel Kaplan, survived the massacre. He was grazed by a bullet and feigned death.

This is how the German witnesses describe the killings in court hearings after the war:

> With the aid of the local police, members of the squadron removed Jewish men from their homes and brought them to the marketplace. In succession, the three platoons led the assembled Jews to the outskirts of town, and 500 to 1,000 yards from the city limits in the open field, the Jews were shot. The three platoons killed their victims in separate locations but in close proximity to each

other. The shooting, by the various platoons, took place in a similar manner. The victims were assembled in groups and marched to the execution place. They stood with their backs to the marksmen; then they were ordered to turn around and face the SS-shooters. Two marksmen aimed and shot the victim from a distance of seven yards. The command to fire was given either by the platoon leaders or the group leaders. As soon as one group of Jews were shot, the marksmen stepped aside, so those who were shot next would fall in succeeding rows. The corpses were not covered with earth. The victims had to wait nearby until their group was brought up and shot. Those who awaited their destiny were able to observe the shooting and hear the rifle salvos.

After the men had all been shot, a member of the SS unit checked the corpses. If he suspected that someone had remained alive, that person was finished off with a "mercy" bullet. At the execution site, the Germans set up machine-gun nests to prevent any apprehended Jews from escaping. Within minutes after the execution, some Gentile peasants descended upon the corpses. Like vultures, they began to strip and pillage the dead.

That ghastly day saw the killings of my father, two uncles, and six cousins. Women and children were spared. My paternal aunt, Malka Reznik, lived next to the marketplace, across from the spot where the Jews were gathered before being marched off to their execution. She recounted to us that she saw my father being led away. As he passed her, he nodded his head in a parting farewell. I cannot even begin to imagine what must have passed through his mind in those final moments. May his memory forever be a blessing.

Many commentaries have been written about the Biblical story of Job, whose suffering and personal losses seemed endless. Throughout tragedy after tragedy, Job never lost his abiding devotion to God. I can equate my Aunt Yentel to Job. In one dreadful moment, she lost her husband, two sons, a son-in-law, a brother, two brothers-in-law, and scores of relatives and friends. When she learned the fate of her husband and children, she went to search for their remains so that she could give them a proper Jewish burial. She was able to locate only the bullet-riddled body of her husband. Amidst her grief, she had the strength to collect the scattered pieces of her husband's skull into her apron, and then bury his remains. Shortly afterward, she learned that her remaining son, daughter-in law, and son-in-law had also perished in a neighboring town. Despite this harrowing catastrophe, she was able to give comfort to her daughters, who had become widows at a very young age. She mourned her overwhelming loss, but never lost faith. She frequently repeated that it was Divine Providence.

There are numerous stories that can be recounted about that fateful day — stories of courage, heroism, betrayal, bestiality, and barbarism. The Germans were able to work with speed and efficiency only because they had help and support from some of the local population. Many Gentiles willingly, and without any coercion, pointed out Jewish homes to the SS, divulged Jewish hiding places, and betrayed people who attempted to conceal their Jewish identity. In one case, an SS officer coaxed and bribed a little Jewish child to reveal his father's hiding place. Ironically, our community was "fortunate," since only adult males were murdered. In neighboring towns, men, women, and children were slaughtered indiscriminately.

The night after the slaughter, many of the women and children found makeshift hiding places. These places ultimately did not provide protection, and the fact that the residents stayed away from their homes made it easier for the local population to plunder abandoned Jewish property. My family spent that night in a crawl space in the woodshed, the same hiding place that had saved my brother. None of us slept that night and I still feel pain and cramps when I recall that experience. There was only enough room to crouch down, and no place to turn. Our refuge abutted the outhouse, and rancid odors permeated the space. At dawn, we came out to face a day of uncertainty, despair, and unending mental anguish.

We spent only one night in our hiding place, but Aron hid behind the woodshed for a long time. His shed lacked even rudimentary sanitary facilities. Food could not be brought to Aron easily; it had to be delivered in a way so as not to arouse suspicion. For nearly three weeks he stayed in this hiding place with room only to sit, stand, and lie down, but no room to exercise. He had little safeguard from the elements, and it rained frequently. While Aron was in his original hiding place, he was not aware that our father had been killed. After three weeks, my brother abandoned the woodshed to hide in the attic of our house. Here he could wash himself, eat more regularly, and interact with us. It was then that he found out that our father was dead.

My mother held on to the faint hope that by some miracle my father was able to escape and would come home alive. As the days passed, however, sadness and grief set in. For over a year after the death of my father, she cried continuously and could not be consoled. My grandmother, Ethel, eventually became resigned to the fact that her daughter, Bashka, son-in law Chaim Neuman, and their daughter, Malka, who lived in the town of Kovel, had also perished. She had one surviving son in Janów, Yankel Reznik, along with his wife Malka, their two boys Yitzchak and Simcha, and a daughter, whose name I have forgotten. Naturally, my grandmother's grief was enormous, but I don't recall seeing her cry. All her pain and grief was kept deep within her heart. Grandma Ethel did not have the best relationship with my mother; yet after my father's death, she chose to live with us, rather then with her surviving son, and at all times she was treated with courtesy and respect.

It was very strange and painful to live in our town immediately after the massacre because of the feelings of despair and bereavement. Never before had a calamity of such proportion befallen our community, and the misery was compounded by the fact that many of the people in the population were related, or at least known to each other. No adult males were in sight for weeks, and no one was sure who was still alive and who was missing. Some of our Christian neighbors took advantage of our plight and tricked Jewish women out of their possessions. Unscrupulous people would approach a Jewish widow or a mother, telling her that her husband or son was in hiding and needed food or clothing to survive. The unfortunate women weren't sure if the information was authentic, but they wouldn't dare refuse the request on the chance that there might be some validity to it.

Rumors abounded. It was said that the Nazis were coming back to finish off the remaining Jews in the town. We expected total annihilation at any given moment. Subsequently, the Germans issued orders stating that all Jews had to register in order to receive rations. This edict forced the rest of the survivors to come out of hiding. People erroneously suspected that the registration rules were just another ploy to draw everyone into the open as a prelude to their destruction. As it turned out, everyone was also issued an identification card. The Jewish cards were marked with a "J" for *Jude* (Jew).

The Germans also decreed that Jews were not allowed to congregate, even for religious services. This rule was very distressing to the many mourners who had religious obligations to recite prayers for family members who had been killed in the massacre. Many of the survivors risked their lives by disobeying the order and reciting the mourner's *Kaddish*, a prayer recited for a deceased person three times a day for a whole year. For a month and a half, no large group services were held, since all adult male survivors were still hiding. But our home was one of many houses where a makeshift synagogue was set up for mourners. Had we been caught holding services, we would have been burned along with our home.

Reciting the mourner's *Kaddish* was enormously painful for me. My mother tried to teach me the words of the prayer, but I simply couldn't bring myself to utter them. She became very angry with me and we both cried during the lesson. To this day, I doubt that she understood the true reason for my reluctance to say the words. She thought I was being disrespectful, but in essence I was expressing my inability to accept my father's death.

The Jewish community was forced to continually pay tribute or bribes to the Germans. To make sure that their demands were met, the Nazis seized a number of Jews as hostages and threatened them with execution unless a certain amount of gold, usually exorbitant, was produced. Torahs were stripped of their ornaments. My mother had to give up her wedding band. Alter Divinski, the chairman of the *Judenrat*, came with other members of his committee to our home to take away her ring. That scene is still vivid in my mind. I remember Mother slipping off the ring, handing it to Divinski, and breaking into sobs. First she lost her husband, and then she had to relinquish the symbol of their marital union.

As time went by, the Jewish townspeople settled down to a life of uncertainty, never sure of what the next day or even the next hour would bring. Somewhere along the way, we learned that Japan had attacked the United States at Pearl Harbor. Then we heard that a state of war existed between Germany and the United States, but this news gave us very little hope. Our reality was that the military situation on the Russian front was rapidly deteriorating, and we learned that the German army had reached the outskirts of Moscow. The prevailing feeling was that Russia would soon surrender, Europe would be under Nazi rule, and at best, we would remain enslaved forever.

In anticipation of another slaughter, many Jews hastily erected secret hideouts. That winter of 1941, I contracted measles and was very ill, and if that was not hard enough to bear, there were rumors that all Jewish inhabitants of my town would be deported and forced to settle in some place in a ghetto. My family was very concerned about my weakened condition and what would lie in store for us all. We tried to manage as best as we could, bartering our possessions to supplement the meager bread rations, performing odd jobs for Gentile neighbors, and providing free labor to the German occupation forces. Occasionally a farmer who had worked for my father would bring us food. For a while my sister Helen worked in the *Komendatur*, the German headquarters. She admitted that she found the *Wehrmacht* soldiers very polite and at times compassionate. Oftentimes they would give her food to take home. Eventually, however, she was forced to give up her job because the Germans decreed that no Jew was allowed to enter the headquarters.

During this agonizing period, there were constant rumors of deportation, impending executions, or resettlement of the Jews to a ghetto (a slum or rundown crowded area of the town surrounded by barbed wire). The inhabitants of the ghetto were not allowed to leave without a permit, and no non-Jew was allowed inside. Throughout the winter, a stream of Jewish refugees who had been expelled from surrounding places that the Germans annexed as part of the Third Reich flowed into our town, further depleting the food supplies. These new Jewish arrivals were not left out in the cold. They were mostly women and children because all the adult males had been killed. The new refugees told us that the Germans had ordered them to abandon their homes, allowing them to bring along only the possessions they could carry on their backs.

CHAPTER 5

Life in the Ghetto

The rumors became a reality. In April of 1942, the order came that the Jews of Janów would, in fact, be evicted from their homes and forced into a ghetto. Just before Passover, a German officer wearing a brown uniform with a Swastika insignia arrived in town. He told the chairman of the Jewish community, Alter Divinski, to take him on a tour of the slums. The snow had just melted and the whole area was a sea of mud. The two men crisscrossed the streets, and at the end of the tour, the German's boots became extremely muddy, so he ordered Mr. Divinski to clean them.

With the holiday approaching, the Jewish community called on the local commandant to ask for the right to bake matzos. For a considerable bribe, permission was obtained. The rabbis granted some dispensations to excuse Jews from following all of the strict dietary laws associated with the holiday. But the holiday that year lacked any joy. It was the first Passover without my father at the Seder (the special meal that takes place on Passover and is conducted during two evenings). On Passover eve, we received the news that in a few days we would have to abandon our homes and move to the slum area.

The designated quarter was not larger than four square blocks. As more Jews from the surrounding towns were resettled there, conditions became impossible. The Nazis conceded and included a number of additional homes within the perimeter of the ghetto when the overcrowding became overwhelming. As soon as it was decreed that we had to move to the ghetto, the German authorities ordered the *Judenrat* to assign a work detail to dig posts and string barbed wire around the enclosure. We were allowed to take with us only what we could carry. As soon as the news spread that the Jews would be resettled, our Christian neighbors approached us, urging us to leave our possessions with them for safekeeping. They all promised that if we were lucky enough to survive the war, we would get our valuables back, but we knew that would not be the case. Those who relinquished their possessions to the Gentiles for safekeeping were at a higher risk of being betrayed to the Nazis, thus assuring that the owners would never claim them back.

Jews from surrounding towns were also forced to abandon their homes and move into our ghetto. Streams of the evicted flowed in from miles around. German documents that surfaced during the postwar war-crimes trials show that the Nazi leaders responsible for the eradication of the Jewish community in Janów allotted living space per person of approximately 1.2 square meters (1 square yard). As the Jews entered the ghetto, the police lined up at the crossing point to check their belongings and sometimes confiscated them. Adjacent to our house lived a kind Gentile family whose son, Senia Lachmai, had become a policeman for the German authorities. Senia spotted one policeman harassing an orphaned Jewish boy who had lost his parents in a house fire in 1940. The policeman was trying to confiscate the child's few possessions. It is hard to believe, but Senia confronted the policeman and stood up for the Jewish boy. The two policemen argued for a long while, but in the end, Senia prevailed.

We were fortunate to have distant relatives, whose family name was Chemerinski, who had a house located within the ghetto. We moved in with them, and at least were assured of a place with a roof. Eight other families joined us. I never saw my childhood home again. We shared the living room with three of the families, which created unimaginable crowded conditions. All told, there were twenty people in one room, and the rest of the house was just as crowded. In this house there were only two husbands; almost everyone else was a widow or child.

Shortly after we moved into the ghetto, a barbed wire fence was strung all around the area and we became isolated from the rest of the town. The fence was high and the wires were thickly intermeshed, making it virtually impossible to crawl through. The windows of the homes facing the outside of the ghetto were boarded up to insure no contact with the outside world, and no one was allowed to walk near the fence or permitted to leave or enter the premises. I felt like a caged animal. I saw Gentile boys outside the ghetto fence playing with my old soccer ball, which had been taken from me. That sight was very upsetting.

There were approximately 3,000 Jews packed into an area of four blocks with, at most, seventy single-story homes. As I indicated, eventually the Germans relented and designated a few other homes for Jews to occupy in another ghetto area that we called *Ripeshczes* (a rundown section of town). The Jews of both ghettos were allowed to mingle with each other during daylight hours. Since the environment was extremely crowded and susceptible to the spread of disease, the Germans ordered all Jews, male and female, to shave their heads. This also served to further denigrate Jewish women.

Despite the fact that our living quarters were extremely tight, with eight families sharing one kitchen, all of us got along quite well. My mother even hired a tutor, a Mr. Brostoff, to enable me to study. She wasn't sure what the future would bring, but she thought that if we survived, at least her youngest son would have an education. She actually traded her own meager rations for a cause that seemed so irrelevant to me at the time.

The *Judenrat* remained as the governing authority in charge of carrying out the mandates of the German government. It administered the affairs of the ghetto and was responsible for distributing rations (which consisted of a little flour), assigning work details, keeping order within the ghetto, and supervising the general welfare of the Jewish community. Work crews were organized by the *Judenrat* to clean up the area and dig a drainage system. It seemed they were preparing the place for a long stay. But the Germans had other plans. To this day I marvel at what was accomplished in that space of time. The most agonizing task for the Jewish administrators, however, came when the Nazis ordered them to provide names of young men who were to be deported to a labor camp. Those who were selected and delivered to the Germans typically were men with little influence in the community.

In the summer of 1942, we planted a garden within the wire fence to supplement our rations. This garden also camouflaged our hiding shelter. My brother, who was forced to work for the Germans in the lumber mill, was once able to barter some valuables for a chicken and smuggled it into the ghetto. The chicken was obviously not properly slaughtered under Jewish religious law. Grandma Ethel, who had continued to live with us, was an extremely religious woman, and so when we sat down to eat, we did not invite her to partake in the meal because we did not want to feed her non-kosher meat. She was very hurt when she saw us eating without her, and she complained to me, "How come I am not invited to the table?" I was sad that she felt left out, but I couldn't divulge the reason she was excluded from the feast. When she finally found out that the chicken was not kosher, she was even more furious.

There was one positive aspect of life in the ghetto. Before we were confined to the ghetto, Jews would rarely dare to congregate, since public gatherings would invite retribution from the German authorities. However, in the ghetto in the evenings after work, young people would socialize, even though it was not permitted. On many evenings, some Gentile boys would also pass through the barbed wire to visit. To them, this was a sport, an adventure. Our complex had many young people living in it, and we always had a large crowd of friends with whom to talk. My oldest sister, Malka, began dating a Jewish boy who had been expelled from Pinsk by the Russians. Because of his family's wealthy status, the Russians considered them undesirable. (His mother was a pharmacist in Janów and his father was killed by the Nazis on August 5, 1941.) People were involved in all kinds of discussions and arguments, ranging from philosophical questions to subjects as frightful as when the ghetto might be liquidated. It makes me extremely sad to think that none of my compatriots survived. There is no telling what contributions all of these people would have made to society had they lived.

In August of 1942, we became aware, through the grapevine, that there were two Ukrainian policemen in Pinsk, referred to as "Number 13" and "Number 41," who were extremely brutal and sadistic. The Jews knew the policemen only by their badge numbers. In the summer of 1942, these policemen were suddenly spotted in our town. It is hard to comprehend how two individuals could strike so much fear in a community. I recall how one of them climbed through the barbed wire into the ghetto, singled out an unsuspecting man, and started beating him with a rubber truncheon. He continued beating him even after the victim grew unconscious. The man was hospitalized, and weeks later still exhibited the bruises and scars.

Right after Rosh Hashanah 1942, we noticed an increased number of Germans whose uniforms were of a different green color from those of the *Wehrmacht*. Based on documents that I have since obtained from Germany, I have now identified them as members of the 2nd Squadron of Mounted Cavalry, Battalion II. We also learned that in the village of Ruck on the outskirts of town, trenches were being dug, presumably as mass graves. The chief German administrator, Lorenz, assured the Jews of Janów that the ditches were to be used only as an underground gasoline storage facility. He gave his "word" that no harm would befall the Jews, since the services the Jews performed were vital to the German economy. Some of us then lived with a sense of false hope that this might be the actual reason for the excavations. But most of the people had a feeling that the end was approaching. Despite our anxiety, there was no attempt at mass escape, even as we learned that other ghettos were being annihilated. In reality, how could 3,000 Jews just disappear?

I believed all hope was lost and that the Jews were resigned to the inevitable. We urged my brother to run away, since, as a young man, he would have the best chance of surviving alone without the burden of a family. Finally, one evening Aron reluctantly agreed to leave the ghetto. I don't remember kissing him goodbye and no one suggested that we all leave. Before dawn, however, Aron returned and stated without any equivocation that he would not escape without the rest of us. My brother never placed his own safety or welfare above that of his family. I recall feeling so very much relieved when Aron returned, for it felt as if our rescuer came back to lead us to freedom. His presence gave me the assurance of not being abandoned and having a better prospect of survival.

CHAPTER 6

The Liquidation of the Janów Ghetto

All able-bodied people in the ghetto were assigned a task. Those who were part of a work detail had to march out as a unit and return with the same group. Stragglers risked being shot. Young boys were also assigned to work, and so I was sent to care for livestock that the Germans had confiscated from the Jews and local peasants. This job gave me the opportunity to leave the ghetto confines and occasionally to have the chance to bring home milk from the cows. On Yom Kippur, it was my turn to graze the cows, but since I wanted to attend *Yizkor* (a Jewish memorial service for the deceased) for my father, I pleaded with a member of the *Judenrat* to excuse me from work. The official from the *Judenrat* heeded my plea and allowed me to skip one turn, as long as I would graze the cattle two days later, on September 24, 1942. That switch in rotation saved my life.

On that day, my sisters Helen and Liza were assigned to pick potatoes in the field adjacent to the lumberyard, while my brother and my eldest sister Malka went to work in the lumber mill. As I tended the cattle, I noticed unusual

German activity on the road leading from the town to the fresh trenches. A policeman stopped by and confided to my working companion, whose last name was Tabachnik, that on the following day the ghetto would be liquidated. He also asked Tabachnik if he had any valuables on him. My first impression was that the policeman was trying to scare us; however, I didn't dismiss what he said as a total fabrication. We went about our chores until it was time to return the livestock to the stalls.

That evening, I learned that all Jews who worked in the lumber mill had been ordered to report for night work and bring three days worth of food. This unusual request heightened my suspicion of impending disaster, so I decided not to return to the ghetto. Instead, I slipped into the lumberyard and luckily found the hiding place my brother had prepared. I had hoped that someone from my family would be there, but I remained there all alone, exhausted, petrified and fearful that I would never again see my family. I eventually fell asleep and spent the whole night with some other townspeople who were also hiding there. On the morning of September 25, Aron learned of my whereabouts, found me, and took me to his new secret location in the lumberyard. It was there that I joined my two sisters, and to my great surprise, my mother, who seemed to have lost her will to survive after my father was killed. Fortunately, Helen and Liza were there because they remained in the lumberyard instead of returning to the ghetto at the end of the day. Mother was in the hiding place because Aron returned to the ghetto to retrieve her. I asked where my other sister, Malka, was, and learned that, tragically, she and Grandma Ethel had not made it out of the ghetto in time.

As Aron and my mother were leaving the ghetto, they saw Malka heading back to our home in the fenced ghetto.

Malka explained that she was going to fetch some clothing for my sisters and shoes for me. Although my mother pleaded with her to flee with them, Malka refused. Malka radiated her characteristic warmth and pensive smile and said that she was so happy that my mother was getting the chance to escape. Later, I learned that Malka's real motive for insisting on returning to the ghetto was her desperate desire to rescue her boyfriend. Unfortunately, soon after she entered the enclosure, the gates were locked and the ghetto was surrounded by Germans and their collaborators. My mother's profound grief over that last glimpse of Malka persisted for the rest of her life. I took Malka's absence rather calmly. Years later, as I reflect on her fate, I am filled with much more pain than I experienced at the moment when I discovered she was missing. Perhaps, at the time, we had a faint hope that she would survive. My mother often spoke with anguish about the tragic moment when she saw Malka, her oldest daughter, for the last time.

On the morning of September 25, 1942, shortly after I was reunited with the remainder of my family in the new hideout, the first column of Jewish men, women, children and infants were taken from the ghetto and marched to their eternal rest. It was difficult for me to believe and comprehend that a community that existed for centuries was being annihilated. The road on which these victims took their last journey passed near the lumberyard. Some men who were in the lumberyard had the courage to climb atop the stacks of lumber and observe the gruesome procession. These men called out, "They're leading a column of people!" The sound of the victims' screams will remain with me forever. The road from the ghetto to the trenches became strewn with Jewish corpses. People who had fallen behind and could not keep up were shot on the spot. The beatings were incessant, and the people were treated worse than a brutish society treats its animals.

When the victims arrived at the pits that had been previously dug in the village called Ruck, they were forced to undress completely, enter the pit, and lie face down. Then they were shot through the neck with submachine guns or rifles. Piles of clothing, stories high, lay strewn on the ground. Several people tried to escape, but very few evaded the hail of machine-gun fire. One act of valor is especially noteworthy. A woman, Chana Gorodetski, was led to execution with her two sons. When a guard hit one of her boys, Chana became enraged and instinctively threw sand in the Nazi's face, calling out, "Children, run!" The disturbance created a distraction and many Jews attempted to get away. In the ensuing shooting most perished, including Chana and one of her children. Her oldest son, Judel, however, was able to escape. He survived and eventually settled in Israel. I also recall the story told by Getzel Shuster, a boy my age, who was taken out of the ghetto and marched to the killing pits. While the victims were still in town, he managed to escape into a courtyard. As he ran through the yard, an elderly Ukrainian woman grabbed him by his hair and held him for the Nazis. Fortunately, he had short hair and was able to pry himself loose and escape. He, too, settled in Israel.

Meanwhile, back in the ghetto, the Germans realized that many Jews were still missing, even after a full day of killing and plundering. So in the evening they set the ghetto on fire. Those who tried to escape the flames were shot. Many chose to perish by fire or smoke inhalation rather than face the muzzles of the German guns. As I previously pointed out, our house in the ghetto had a hiding place under our garden. The entrance to the hiding area was accessed from the basement, and was very ingeniously disguised. A large hole had been excavated and a ceiling placed over the hole. Soil was placed over the boards, and vegetables planted on top. In this house, there also lived with us a young couple with a small baby. When we planned our hideout, we knew that any noise would frighten the child and she could betray all of us. Therefore, a second hiding place was constructed for the parents and the child. This place was also well camouflaged, but predictably the gunfire and noise outside was too frightening for the baby. She began to cry, and her wailing alerted the Nazis. Unfortunately the family was doomed.

During the liquidation of the ghetto, Judel Shuster, a boy from Janów, hid in our shelter along with my sister and grandmother and some other people who lived in our house. He escaped from the hideout after the ghetto was set afire, and he later informed my family that our house was the last one to go up in flames. He told us that when the Germans set our house on fire, my grandmother remained inside the hiding place and perished, while my sister, her boyfriend, and the rest of the young people escaped the burning building. Those who surrendered while the ghetto was in flames were assembled near the *Judenrat* building, and some of them were tossed into the pyre alive. The rest, including Malka and her boyfriend, were gunned down during their attempted escape. That night, the fire that consumed the buildings in the ghetto, along with its inhabitants, illuminated the skies. Out of the whole group of people who were in the hiding place in my house, only Judel Shuster survived.

Before the ghetto was liquidated, the chairman of the *Judenrat*, Alter Divinski, was informed that the Jews of the ghetto would be killed. He returned to the ghetto, bloodied, and cried out, "Jews hide! This is the end!" But it was in vain and too late.

The brutality that took place before the victims were killed was unimaginable and inhuman. The Nazis who witnessed the killing described the family separation at the execution site as heartwrenching. Jews were forced to enter the pits, and those who refused were brutally whipped. The narrative that follows is an excerpt from a transcript of the trial of an SS Nazi, Adolf Petsch, who was one of the executioners. The accused Petsch described the shooting of the Jews in the following manner:

> To the Aktion in Janów, according to my recollection, three of us were assigned as marksmen. Before the executions in Yanow, the Jews were forcibly gathered within the ghetto. Those who hid were searched and found. In this connection, I somehow recall that during the search for concealed Jews, even hand grenades were used.
>
> From the assembly place the Jews were marched 2 km. to the killing location on the outskirts of the town. If I recall correctly, during this campaign either the Order Police or the Gendarmes were deployed for action. The required pits were already excavated, but I have no idea who made the arrangement. Possibly the excavation was ordered by the area Territorial Commissioner. We shot all the Jews who were lying in the pits through the neck with submachine guns and single shots. For this task, we who did the shooting stood inside the pits. Before they were shot, the Jews had to undress outside the pits. Men, women and children were killed. With respect to the total count of those who were killed then, I can't give you the exact number. It could have been 1,000, 1,500, or only 800. It can be stated

with certainty that there were many hundreds. Before their liquidation, the Jews were forced to surrender their valuables. I can't say with certainty who was responsible for collecting those things; however, I am inclined to believe that someone who belonged to the District Command was entrusted with it. The members of the District Command wore brown uniforms, and we named them there and then 'golden pheasants.'

In the course of the shootings in Yanow, it is obvious we came across scenes, especially when mothers and children, so to say nursing babies, had to be killed. In those cases it was arranged that the children were shot before the mothers, to prevent the children from generating even louder screams. According to my recollection of that time, the killing in Yanow lasted from 8:00 or 8:30 AM until approximately 2:00 PM. During the liquidation campaign, no alcohol was distributed. Only after we returned to our posts were drinks dispensed. To complete my description of the killing in Yanow, I must amplify that the three of us took turns during the shootings. The three of us did the shooting from morning until the afternoon.

The victims had to lie facing the earth before they were shot. Eventually the assembled who were standing next in line to be executed were forced to lie face down on top of the corpses. We, ourselves, have never stood on top of the dead people during the shooting. When the pit was almost full, the victims had to stand at the rim of the pit, and as they were shot they fell into it. When it came to shooting mothers with small babies, it was explained to the mothers that they had to place the children next to them, and to keep the children secure next to them. The babies' heads had to be unobstructed to avoid any 'difficulty' during the shooting. Otherwise the children may not have been killed. In no case was it actually ascertained whether the victims were dead. That was also not our responsibility. It is within the realm of possibility that some remained alive. I don't know who covered the pits. If by chance some had remained alive they were also buried.

During the whole Aktion we did not eat; we only smoked. We could not eat at all because a penetrating odor permeated the area. It smelled from blood and excrements because of the victims who lost their bowels during the killing. After participating in these activities, my uniform was soaked with blood and my hands were also smeared with blood. This was true with all those who had to do the shooting. I, as did the other marksmen, received a new uniform after every shooting. Whether it was a washed uniform or a different one, I don't know. To the SS men it was quite clear the orders were correct; therefore, no second thought was given to the matter. The orders existed, and we had to carry them out. We were chosen to shoot and we had to do it.

CHAPTER 7

Cleaning Up the Lumber Mill

The following morning, September 26, 1942, the *Einsatz Kommando* killing squads, having annihilated the Janów ghetto, now approached the lumber mill. The Jews hiding at the mill thought the Germans were passing on their way to board a train, since the railroad station was just across the way. But we were mistaken. Initially, only a small detachment entered the mill, while the rest of the Nazis remained outside. The director of the mill ordered all workers to assemble in the courtyard. Most of the males, including my brother Aron complied, while all the females and I remained hidden. The Gentile workers were ordered to leave the assembly place, and Jewish workers were commanded to remain. The gate of the lumber mill swung open and a swarm of Nazis came in. Suddenly, we heard a disturbing commotion outside, with shouts of "They came to kill us!" Fortuitously, Aron ran away and joined us in the hideout.

We quickly realized that we were being rounded up again, and that the storm troopers were going to finish the job they had started the day before to ensure that there were no survivors. People ran for cover, but some who had lost their families the preceding day simply lost their will to survive. Those woeful people just stood there, waiting for the inevitable. Nine of us quivered in fear in our hiding place — my family of five and some other friends. Shouts of *"Ferfluchte Juden, heraus!"* — "Damned Jews, come out!" — echoed around us. One of the men hiding with us got up and tried to leave the hideout, but fortunately someone grabbed him and shoved him back. As I watched that man get up, I was positive that we had been discovered. The only thought that crossed my mind at that split second was that the end had come for us.

I have relived that moment many times in my life. I felt as if the mass of my body had settled in my legs, making them strangely anchored to the ground. My mind went completely blank. After a while, all the blood rushed to my head. All of us were inches away from certain death. We recognized the voices of people we knew being forced to abandon their hideouts and walk to the assembly place. There must have been a holding area for the Jews who were apprehended near our hideout, since we heard a great deal of activity and people crying very close by. Not having eaten for an extended time, I was overcome with enormous hunger. My sister Liza had such a craving for water that it almost drove her to insanity, and she attempted to run out of the hiding place. Finally, Helen licked Liza's lips to relieve her overbearing thirst.

Two other episodes on that day also remain etched in my mind. In an adjoining hideout, a woman, Mrs. Einbinder, and her two children, were discovered. The fact that she spoke Russian to her captor indicated that he was not a German policeman. She told her captor that she was not hiding, but simply sleeping there. She also tried to impress upon him that her daughter was a friend of a Gentile boy in town. I found it ironic that at that moment, facing certain death, the woman had hoped her executioners would be impressed with her story. They were not.

I remain haunted by the second episode, a conversation I overheard between a young Jewish girl and her German captor. I can still hear the poor teenager's cries and remember her exact words as she cried and begged the Nazi to spare her. *"Mein lieber Herr, Ich bin sehr jung, Ich habe angst, Ich will nicht sterben."* "My dear Sir, I am very young, I am frightened, I don't want to die," the poor child implored. The Nazi soldier tried to console her. In a calm and dispassionate manner, he said, *"Hab kein angst, es dauert nicht lang, wir benutzen machine Gewehr"* – "Don't be afraid, this won't take long, we use machine guns." I also recollect one of the Ukrainian guards, walking on top of our shelter and whistling the Russian tune, *"Shiroka Strana Moja Rodnaya,"* a tune exalting the greatness of the Soviet motherland.

The Nazis swarmed around us like hunters, removing layers of boards from the stacks of lumber searching for their prey. Suddenly the victims who had been apprehended were ordered to rise, and all were led away. The victims' screams became unbearable. When they were gone, the silence that followed can truly be described as deadly. The stillness gave us some hope that the hunt was over. For the moment we had survived. We remained in our hideout, surrounded by total silence. The thought entered our minds that we might be the sole survivors of the whole community — the only Jews left alive. The feeling of despair and the thoughts that raced through my mind cannot possibly be put into words. We had been saved for the moment, but we had no idea of what our next move should be. We only realized that other Jews remained alive when we heard a voice cry out, *"Shma Yisrael,"* "Hear O Israel, we have come back."

Jews who were rounded up in the lumberyard were lined up, and a selection process took place. Men with an essential trade were spared a while longer, and the rest were marched off naked to be executed. The Germans spared the life of one young Jewish girl named Esther Lederman. It is hard to believe, but these barbaric Nazis were captivated by her beauty, and decided to let her live.

I have since learned some details from the survivors of that group who were in the lumberyard. At the assembly place, all the victims were ordered to undress. The Nazis then called out the names of those people whom the director of the mill, an ethnic German, had chosen to save. As the name of an essential worker was called out, the individual would come forward and kneel in the designated location. If the person whose name was called did not respond immediately, some other man who had the sense in that split second to assume his identity would walk to the side. After the selection process was completed, those who remained were marched to their graves. The manager of the mill gave the survivors a pep talk. He urged them to work hard as a token of appreciation for having been spared. These workers were allowed to retrieve their clothing from the pile left behind before they returned to the lumberyard.

There were also a handful of Jews from the ghetto who were spared, who worked in essential trades, including physicians, nurses, pharmacists, and other skilled workers vital for providing services to the town. Eventually all those who the Nazis let live were placed in a small ghetto, consisting of two houses surrounded by barbed wire. They were promised protection as long as they were willing to work for the Germans. The Nazis may also have used these Jews as bait to lure other survivors back to town. Many survivors had fled to the forest, but some could not adjust to life there. The bait seemed to work, since a number of Jews did return to Janów and were then killed. The "essential" Jews were allowed to live until non-Jewish replacements were found. Six weeks after the first massacres, they, too, were executed.

CHAPTER 8

The Escape

After an exhausting and traumatic day, we fell asleep on the evening of September 26. During the night, we were awakened by a kind Ukrainian guard who had overheard someone snoring. He told us that the sentry would be changing soon and that we would have to be quiet to avoid detection. He suggested that we leave the hiding place and join up with the Jews who had been deemed essential and who had, therefore, been spared the day before. I don't know why the guard let us go. No doubt, he had taken part in that very roundup. Perhaps he was remorseful and was seeking absolution. The men in our hideout took his advice and joined some survivors in a shack in the lumberyard, while the women and I stayed behind for the rest of the night. Aron then came back for my sisters and secretly led them to where other survivors were housed.

The day after the slaughter in the lumberyard, all the remaining "essential" men were ordered to report for work. My brother and the others were ordered to load logs onto flatcars destined for Germany. My mother and I remained in hiding. I felt forlorn, not having eaten in days, and I felt cut off, wondering if I would be rescued. We could not move around since there were Ukrainian guards posted throughout the lumberyard. I presented a unique problem because all the other Jewish children had been killed, and my presence could not be explained. Finally, on the evening of September 27, my mother and I were spirited out of the hideout and taken to the lumberyard shack. I soon learned that the hiding place where I had spent that first night had been discovered, and that all those still hiding there perished. During the night I stayed in the lumber mill shack, and the next day Aron hid me in different places throughout the yard. It is clear to me now that the authorities, as well as the guards, knew that many Jews were still hiding in the lumberyard. At one particular time, I had to go to the bathroom, and in the doorway I saw a guard flirting with a Jewish girl. My brother and I passed him without issue. It seems that once the majority of Jews of the ghetto and lumberyard were liquidated, there were no immediate plans to go on with the killing.

On September 28, 1942, my brother determined that we needed to escape to the forest of Zawishcze, the same forest where we once had played and roamed freely. It is difficult to describe the effort and logistics that went into extricating me from the lumber mill. That morning, Aron took me out from the shack, and with the help of other survivors, who served as lookouts, smuggled me into an outhouse, where I was told to lock the door, and there I remained until dark. It was an incredibly frightening experience, at the age of twelve, to stay locked up for the entire day in that outhouse while people, including some of the Ukrainian guards, tried to use the toilet. I was scared to death that I would be discovered. Once again I felt abandoned, and when Aron came to visit me, I cried in sheer desperation, asking why he had rescued me in the first place only to leave me all alone. Throughout that time, from the day I left the ghetto through my hiding in the lumber mill, there was nothing to eat and very little to drink.

While I was locked in the outhouse, my brother made preparations to smuggle my mother and my sister Liza out of the lumberyard. His plan was to disguise them as peasants. As I mentioned before, at times Gentile boys would sneak under the barbed wire to congregate with the Jewish boys and girls. One of the boys, Gora Kulich, was in love with a Jewish girl who was killed when the ghetto was liquidated. He felt a tremendous personal loss and kinship with the surviving Jews. This boy risked his life to provide peasant outfits for my mother and sister. Years later, I learned Gora was killed by the Nazis. Outside the lumber mill gate, Jews loaded logs on flat cars. To help my mother and sister escape, the workers created some diversionary noise to distract the Ukrainian guards' attention, and at that moment my mother and Liza were able to slip away from the lumber mill undetected. They then proceeded toward the Zawishcze forest, where they hoped to find refuge.

Mother and Liza planned ultimately to head toward Potapowicz, a village near the forest, and, if they got that far, they would then contact a farmer, Radion Naumchik, who once worked for my father. They intended to inform Radion that Aron, Helen, Shlomo Weiss, and I would follow the next day. Shlomo Weiss was my sister Helen's boyfriend. He came from a well-to-do family from Janów, and their economic status made them a target of the state. Consequently, his parents and siblings had been deported to Siberia on June 21, 1941; however, Shlomo eluded the Soviet police that day. The following day, the Germans invaded Russia, Shlomo was trapped, and thus had to endure the German occupation.

My mother and Liza left in the middle of the day and proceeded toward the forest, approximately ten miles from the town. They walked the total distance in broad daylight, traversing two villages before they reached *Kanal Krulewski* (the Dnepro-Bug Canal), a waterway outside the village of Potapowicz. No bridge spanned the river, making a ferry or private boat the only means of crossing. They reached the river at dusk and decided to lay low in the marshes, since they had seen a policeman on the shore. The two hid until dark, but by then the ferry had ceased operating. They were exhausted, and not knowing what to do, fell asleep. Although they were disguised, someone must have recognized them and word that they were alive soon reached the village of Potapowicz. The ferryboat captain, Ochrim, who knew my family, heard about it, and set out to look for them that evening. He called out: *"Baby, Baby"* (Ladies, Ladies) to get their attention. Mother and Liza heard his call, but were too frightened to reveal themselves. Nevertheless, Ochrim left a boat for them to use. Mother and Liza scouted the riverbank and were fortunate to find it, and thus were able to cross to the far bank. They proceeded to Radion's house, but did not dare wake him; instead, they stayed on his porch until daybreak. At daybreak, Radion invited them into his house and hid them for several hours. He also gave them provisions. Liza mentioned to him that the rest of our group would be crossing the river the following night and he advised the ferryboat captain to leave a boat for us as well. Liza and Mother then proceeded into the forest.

That same day, at the end of the work shift, my brother, along with Shlomo Weiss and Helen, remained outside the gate and hid under logs instead of returning to the lumber mill shack. In the evening, my brother removed me from the outhouse and we joined Helen and Shlomo. During the night, we slipped out of our hiding place and proceeded toward the forest. We avoided the main road, walking through the fields and woodlands in the hope of avoiding detection. At one point we were lost, and stopped at a farmer's house to ask for directions and water. Although the farmer knew we were Jewish, and his son-in-law was a policeman who had helped round up Jews in Janów, he put us on the right course and wished us well.

Toward dawn we reached the canal and found ourselves in an open field. We, too, hid in the marshes. In the distance we could see a policeman on a bicycle crossing the river by ferry. It was utterly depressing to realize that we had come so far and yet were unable to go any further. We stayed in the marshes a full day, and in the evening, my brother and Shlomo scouted for a way to traverse the river. We found the boat that either Radion or the ferry captain, Ochrim, had cached for us. But we still didn't know if Mother and Liza had made it across to the forest or if they had been caught.

After we crossed the river, we quickly scurried into the forest to hide. Aron went to see Radion to find out the fate of Mother and Liza, while Helen, Shlomo, and I hid in the forest on the outskirts of the village. Radion told Aron where to find Mother and Liza. He was also kind enough to give us some provisions. It was the first time in days that I had eaten an adequate meal. We then trudged deeper into the forest of Zawishcze, close to my old home, which was where Radion told us we could find Mother and Liza. The weather had become sultry and hot and we were extremely thirsty. We finally found my mother and sister, along with a few other survivors from our town. There was no clean water, so we were forced to drink from a stagnant creek. Shortly after, my brother contracted amebic dysentery and was ill for a long time.

We were anxious to join up with the Russian partisans. These were primarily bands of Russian soldiers who were unable to break out of the German encirclement, or former Russian soldiers who escaped from labor camps. But, shockingly, they rejected us. The partisans immediately began to berate the Jews as cowards who were led to slaughter without putting up any resistance. They accused the men of being lowly merchants, incapable of carrying arms or fighting. We had originally believed that if we could reach the forest, our problems would be solved. Now we were deeply disappointed and it was an enormous letdown. The first Jew from Janów to die in the forest at the hands of the partisans was a teenager named Ethel Birenboim. She was taken by a group of partisans to their barracks and used for sexual gratification. Eventually they shot her, since they claimed that Ethel had a venereal disease. As it turned out, she was merely menstruating.

CHAPTER 9

Life in the Forest

For a few days after arriving in the forest I was euphoric. I had survived! However, the danger and hardships soon became apparent. The realization that my oldest sister was dead also set in. Over the next two weeks, a few more survivors arrived in the forest. The boy named Judel Shuster, who had hidden with my sister and grandmother in the ghetto, was one of them. He was the last person to have seen my sister Malka alive, and was among the Jews who had assembled in front of the burning *Judenrat* building. He told us how one woman berated the Germans for their heinous deeds, and as a punishment, was tossed into the flames alive. I never asked him how he escaped. Once, while I was sitting by a fire with Aron and Judel, reminiscing about Malka, Aron remarked to Judel in a very sad tone, "If only you could have rescued her." I know that there were periods in my life, after escaping from the ghetto that I envied the dead. And now over the last few years, I have been able to reflect a great deal on the events surrounding Malka's life and death. My thoughts have often focused on her last moments. I still wonder how and where she perished. Was she apprehended and shot? Was she killed during her escape, or possibly burned alive? Obviously the answers are lost forever.

Some of the Jewish survivors who hid in the woods had difficulty coping with the harsh conditions in the wild. Judel stayed in the forest for about two weeks, and then returned along with Yacov Divinski, the son of the chairman of the *Judenrat*, to Janów, to join the remaining survivors in the small ghetto that the Germans created to incarcerate the "essential" Jews who were spared. The loss of his family and his inability to cope with the difficulties of life in the forest were more than Judel could tolerate. As I pointed out, eventually all of those remaining survivors in the town were executed.

Many of the refugees in the forest built their shelters close to the road and took too many foolish chances. The smoke from their fires could be seen for miles and was usually a dead giveaway. The Germans often ventured into Zawishcze. We could hear their trucks and motorcycles day and night, passing our shelter. It would have been so easy to ambush them if only we had the experience and weapons. Oftentimes the Nazis would drive into the forest in trucks, blazing away with their machine guns not far from our refuge. I suspect they knew our general location but were too frightened to venture deeper into the forest for fear of being ambushed by the partisans.

Our hiding place in the forest was on part of the estate owned by the Polish nobleman Graff Poslawski. During the Russian occupation, he fled the country, and his castle was converted first into a youth hostel and then into a home for the elderly. When the Germans came, most of the elderly moved away, but those who had no place to go remained behind. Poslawski had many servants, one of whom was a custodian who had lost his job during the Russian occupation. When the Germans occupied the palace, the former custodian was under the impression that the care of the castle remained his responsibility. The custodian, who was extremely sadistic, dug a pit and placed inside it an old Jewish woman who remained in the castle. The brutal man kept her there without any food or water and she lingered there until she died. There were a handful of elderly folk still in the castle when we reached the forest. That winter, a German reconnaissance party entered their lodgings and killed them all. Later on, when these "soldiers" returned to their posts in Pinsk, they reportedly bragged that they had hunted down and killed many partisans.

We arrived in the forest at the end of September, and the weather was warm, so sleeping outdoors was no problem. When it rained, we found shelter and protection under the dense foliage. In October, it became quite cool, especially at night. The trees began to lose their leaves, and it was progressively more difficult to hide. At first, we built a tent out of hay to provide some protection from the elements. When it grew even colder, we kept a fire going at all times and slept around it. However, any part of our bodies away from the fire remained cold. I had a habit of taking off my boots and sitting barefoot at the fire. I wanted to give my feet a rest, since I kept the boots on without changing my socks or washing my feet. My mother always admonished me to keep my boots on in case we had to escape in a hurry. Needless to say, we lived in squalor. We had only the clothing we escaped in, with no changes of underwear. We rarely bathed and consequently we became infested with lice. Every seam in our garments that touched our bodies had nests of lice. To get rid of the infestation, we would hold our undershirts over the flame, and as the smoke and heat rose, the shirt would unfurl and the insects and eggs would die. Unfortunately, at times a garment would catch fire and go up in flames along with the lice.

As previously stated, the survivors were not prepared and lacked the experience to cope with outdoor life. They made too much noise, left visible tracks, and were not cautious. Eventually this problem led to tragic consequences. One day, a group of young men went to obtain provisions in the village of Chomichevo. One of them, Leizer Ratnofski, was overpowered by a farmer, who tied him up and alerted the Germans. The villagers didn't dare untie the man for fear of a German reprisal. When Leizer did not return, we correctly assumed that he had been captured. Immediately, we abandoned our encampment. We knew that the Germans would torture him into revealing where the rest of us were hiding. As it happened, he led them to the forest; but when he and the Germans arrived there, he either bolted from the wagon and was shot in flight, or changed his mind at the last moment and refused to cooperate. A search party later located his mutilated body. To the Russian partisans' perception, this incident was further proof that Jews couldn't be trusted.

CHAPTER 10

The Ambush

During the first two months of life in the forest, we changed our location four or five times. At some point, we acquired a horse and sled. With the approach of winter, though, it became clear that we had to construct some form of underground shelter to keep us warm and provide us a degree of security. At the end of November, we chose a location for our first underground shelter in a place we thought was safe. Other Jewish survivors hid nearby in two additional shelters. Our refuge was the closest to the main road. One day in mid November 1942, with the construction of the shelter not totally finished, and temperatures inside very cold, I sat warming myself at an outdoor fire with my sister Liza. I heard noises and conversations coming from the road. The road was obscured by a shelter built of hay. My sister went to see who was coming and at that instant I heard gunfire and shouts in German of "*Halt!*" I bolted toward the underground shelter where my mother and some others were hiding, and without looking back screamed, *"Germans, Germans!"* Then I kept running.

There was snow on the ground and I found it difficult to run with my boots on, so I took them off and continued barefoot. I dropped one boot but had the sense to turn around and pick it up. Had I not done so, I would undoubtedly have suffered irreversible frostbite later on. As I ran, bullets flew all around me, and people scattered in all directions. Some survivors became confused and, not knowing where the shots were coming from, ran directly into the ambush. We were fortunate that the forest was dense and the tree trunks thick enough to block most of the bullets. Luckily, I was able to join up with my sister, Helen, and a group of five other survivors. That evening, we were hit with a blizzard that lasted the whole night. The seven of us huddled together on the ground without any protection from the elements. I longingly wondered if Mother, Liza, and Aron were alive.

The human character is put to the supreme test during such adverse conditions. Some people respond nobly, while others lose reverence for their fellow men, as this anecdote will demonstrate. While we were huddled under the open skies, my pretty sister Helen asked a man in the group if he would share his fur coat with me. That contemptible man retorted that he was willing to share his coat only with her, and no one else. Despite the wind and snow, we actually fell asleep. The snow finally stopped, the sun began to shine, and then we realized that we had no idea where we were. The snow hid the road and trails, and we walked in circles all day long. The fear, cold, hunger, and exhaustion were overwhelming. We knew that we were near our shelter, but since the snow covered the whole terrain, there were no visible landmarks or trails.

While we were wandering around, an event occurred that still haunts me. We spotted an object on the bank of a river. As we drew nearer, it became apparent that the object was a child, a little boy of about eight or nine years of age, whose last name was Pizman. He was a survivor from our town and escaped from the ghetto all alone, and attached himself to a family of four brothers and a niece and nephew. They had shared a room in the ghetto with the Pizman family. These brothers, though no relation, were like me, named Reznik. Young Pizman was lying on the snow in shorts, barely alive, but still conscious. He had run out of the shelter, gotten lost, and was too exhausted to run anymore. We stopped and told him that we would send help. He did not cry or beg us to take him along, but merely nodded his head as if to say, "What choice do I have?" Though I don't know what we could have done for him, I still feel as if we abandoned him. On the other hand, we did not know where we were going and could barely fend for ourselves.

We also came across two frozen bodies that day. They were the bodies of partisans — one was a Russian Jew named Sasha Berkovitz, the other was Misha, who had fought in the Spanish Civil War. These men had been respected leaders within the Russian partisan movement and were very decent individuals. With their loss, we survivors lost true friends and the moderating influence within the partisan movement. Since their weapons were gone, we knew that the Germans had found them. (Earlier on in the fall, they had spent a number of occasions with my family around the fire.)

Toward evening we spotted footsteps in the snow and followed the trail, though we were not quite sure where it would lead. As we continued walking, we came across a familiar landmark and realized where we were. We had come to an abandoned forest ranger's home, not far from our underground shelter. It was the same house where my brother had tried to obtain lumber for the underground shelter. The abandoned house had a garden and we found some frozen cabbage and tried to eat it, but even after two days of wandering, exhaustion, and hunger, I found the frozen vegetable considerably unpalatable.

After an exhausting day of wandering, we reached the location of our original base camp, and observed with horror that the Nazis had set fire to our lodgings. We approached the place with great fear and trepidation wondering what might be found there — perhaps Germans waiting in ambush, or a corpse of someone from our group. I feared that my mother might have perished inside the shelter when it was set on fire or that she might have been shot while escaping. I didn't have the faintest hope that she survived. To my great relief, I saw no dead people at the campsite. We saw footprints in the snow, which gave us the hope that someone was looking for us.

We didn't want to start a fire at night for fear of attracting the enemy's attention. Once again my hunger and thirst were almost unbearable, and despite the fear that the Germans had poisoned the well nearby, we drank from it. By the end of the day, a great deal of snow had gotten into our garments and footwear. Little by little, the snow started melting. As we sat down, the moisture began to freeze up and icicles formed in our shoes. That evening, we decided to split up into two parties. Some remained at the campsite, while Helen, the man who refused to share his coat with me, and I set out in search of the other Jewish survivors, who were hiding about five miles away. By following the tracks in the snow, we proceeded to the other camp though we did not know if anyone was still alive there.

We slept outdoors for another night and were able to burrow into a haystack to keep warm. In the morning, we picked up the trail. Luckily we met up with a fellow survivor who was looking for his wife and children who had escaped with us during the ambush. The man informed us that my family was alive and that Shlomo, Helen's boyfriend, had been wounded in both arms. When we were finally all reunited, we were most thankful. Everyone had doubted that Helen and I remained alive. By the same token, I had no hope that Liza, who had been in the direct line of fire, or Mother, who was so frail, would ever be able to survive. Unfortunately, six men had died in the raid.

We then informed the Reznik brothers about little Pizman. They immediately went in search of him. When the youngster was picked up after approximately 48 hours of exposure, he was still alive, but his knee was severely affected by frostbite. Gangrene eventually set in, emitting a stench from the decaying flesh that was horrendous. The boy suffered and lingered on for about two months, and he eventually died of toxemia. I believe that at the time of his death, he was only 10 years old. Shortly before he died, Pizman was said to have uttered, "After the war, they will remove my bad leg and fit me with an artificial limb and no one will be able to know the difference." When he died, there was no member of his family to mourn him. May his memory forever be a blessing.

What follows are the details of how my family survived the ambush. During the German attack in the forest, my mother, Shlomo Weiss, and the rest of the inhabitants in the underground shelter heard my shouts and tried to escape. Unfortunately, one man from our hiding place was killed outright, and Shlomo was shot in both arms. Despite losing function in both of his hands, lacking first aid, and losing blood, he made his way to the village of Simchovitch. There he stopped at the home of a peasant who had worked for my father. The man recognized Shlomo and urged him to run away, since the Germans who had ambushed the survivors during the day were now in the village. The man told him how to escape without detection. Shlomo was able to make his way back to the forest and found refuge with other remaining survivors. For nearly 24 hours, though, Shlomo bled and received no aid. There were no analgesics for his pain or sterile dressings for his wounds. For several months, he had no function in either of his arms, so he had to be assisted with all of his basic needs. For example, it was extremely difficult for him to scratch himself. This presented an enormous problem since proper hygiene was impossible. I remember having to scratch his itches. As the months passed, he remarkably regained complete use of one of his hands.

Though Helen and I were together after the ambush, we were still separated from the rest of our family. All along, I had the feeling that my brother was alive, since he hadn't been with us when we were attacked. Just before the Nazi ambush, he had gone to get some material for our shelter from a house that was being demolished, and he had taken the horse and sled with him. As I was escaping, I saw the horse and sled returning to the campsite without Aron. I concluded that when the shooting started, Aron must have realized what was happening and run for cover. I later learned that, while the Germans fired in his direction, Aron had managed to jump from the sled and hide in a ditch.

Mother and Liza's escape was even more miraculous. My mother had a severe asthma attack shortly before the ambush. When she heard my screams and rifle fire, she stepped aside to give some younger people a chance to break out. She was dressed in a long heavy coat and could not run, so she simply fell down in the brush a few feet away from the shelter and waited for nightfall. Of all the people who were with my mother in the underground shelter, she was the only one who survived that raid unscathed. The night of the ambush, after darkness set in, she picked herself up and started walking in what she perceived to be toward the direction of the village of Potopavicz. She was alone and believed that her whole family had been wiped out that afternoon. Because she cared very little about what would happen to her, she decided to walk to the village and surrender to the Germans. When Mother came to the main road, however, she actually took a turn that led her in the opposite direction from the village. She was a lonely, dejected woman walking in the dark night. The wind was whipping and the snow was pilling up. She tripped and fell, yet somehow summoned the strength to go on.

There is no way to imagine the despair and anguish she felt that night. My mother was following wagon wheel tracks when she suddenly heard a command in Russian, telling her to stop and identify herself. At that point she didn't care about living, and proceeded to reveal her identity to the sentry. Soon two men came toward her and realized that she was not a threat. By complete chance, my mother had stumbled upon the encampment of Russian partisans. The camp was located off the main road in a secluded area of the forest. I can only conclude that some supernatural power hovered over her, guiding her toward that destination. The partisans could not comprehend how she arrived there, and were suspicious of her presence. Nevertheless, she was taken inside the compound.

During the ambush, my sister Liza, who was with me at the fire, fell to the ground when the first shots rang out. For a time she lay motionless on the snow, and then the shooting subsided. After a while, she heard someone say in Russian, "This girl is dead." My sister cautiously opened one eye to see who it was and then she heard another person say, "She is still alive; she must be wounded." When she opened both eyes, she realized that the men were part of a partisan reconnaissance unit, and one of them was Jewish. The partisans did not want to be burdened with a Jewish girl, so they left and went off to determine the location of the German party. When Liza tried to follow them, one turned a gun on her and threatened to kill her if she followed them. When the reconnaissance party finally returned to their base camp and unit, they found my mother and informed her that they had found a girl alive where our camp was attacked. By their description of the girl's eyes, my mother knew it was Liza.

At the campsite after the ambush, Liza had called out, "Is anyone alive?" When no one responded she decided to go to Potopavicz to seek refuge with one of the villagers. The snow had obscured the road and she was unsure of where to go, but she found her way to the riverbank. At that point the rags that covered her legs fell off, so she was forced to walk in the snow barefoot. As she made her way to the village, Liza met a band of Gypsies who had heard the shooting and were also hiding in the forest, so she joined up with them. The Gypsies returned to their campground and found the camp intact. They lit a fire and when Liza tried to warm herself, the female Gypsies refused to allow her to sit by the fire. It was only after they fell asleep that she was able to warm herself. By then her feet were frostbitten and she felt a great deal of pain.

In the morning, the Gypsies put their wives and children in wagons and left camp. Liza followed the wagons on foot. Suddenly they encountered men with rifles behind the trees. The men ordered the caravan to stop and asked them for identification. Their reply was, "We are poor Gypsies." At that point, Liza realized that the armed men were not Germans, since the Gypsies were not frightened. Someone called out, "Are all of you Gypsies?" Liza admitted that she was Jewish. The very same partisan who turned the gun on her when she wanted to follow him, informed her that Mother was safe. Liza and Mother were soon reunited. Ironically, when the Germans ambushed us, Liza and Mother had played dead a short distance from each other, and despite the fact that Liza called out to the survivors, Mother did not hear her.

The partisans were faced with a dilemma regarding the arrival of Mother, Liza, and the Gypsies because they knew the location of the partisans' camp. The partisans did not want to keep them, but they feared that if they let them go, they might reveal their hideout to the Germans. On previous occasions, those who had accidentally stumbled onto a partisan camp had been shot. According to my mother and sister, the commander of the partisans took a liking to the Gypsy children, and as a result, they were all spared. After four or five days, Mother and Liza were escorted from the partisan encampment to the shelter where the rest of us were hiding. Helen and I told the partisans where they could find the remains of their fallen comrades. I felt very lucky and grateful for the new gift of life, and felt fortunate that my family was together again.

In time we learned how the Germans had discovered our location. My father had had an employee who was a Ukrainian nationalist and a former fighter with the White Army in the Ukraine. (These Ukrainian soldiers were loyal to the Czar and fought against the Soviet regime.) He and his wife did not get along with the other employees, and my father had tried to fire him. After a protracted labor-relations hearing, my father won the case and the man was evicted. When this Ukrainian worker learned about our hideout, he betrayed us by leading the Germans to our underground shelter. Ultimately, the partisans shot him for his treachery.

CHAPTER 11

Living Underground

After the ambush, we remained in our new shelter with approximately thirty-five other survivors. Our food had been burned and the Jews at this campsite had very little to share. We slaughtered two beautiful horses for meat. Killing the horses was a traumatic experience. They were clobbered on the head with a metal object; however, it took a very long time before the animals succumbed. When the horsemeat ran out, we had to take a risk and scour the neighboring villages for food. At times, the Germans would wait in the village to ambush a Jew, or a villager would deliver a survivor to them for a bounty.

One night, three of the four Reznik brothers, who were not related to us, left to seek food in the village of Potapowicz. When they didn't return by morning, we realized they must have been apprehended. Two of the brothers indeed had been captured, and the third was wounded but managed to escape. The Nazis tortured their captives, demanding that they reveal the hideout of the remaining Jews. The young men — who were known to be very tough — never betrayed the rest of us although their bones were crushed during the interrogation. A local policeman from Janów was with the Nazis and was alleged to have said to the Germans that they would never break the spirit of the brothers. In the morning, the brothers were dragged outside and shot. The wounded brother who had escaped was spotted by a group of partisans. They demanded a password. He had no way of knowing it, and was shot as an enemy. While this was taking place in Potapowicz, those of us who remained in the hideout were on heightened alert, since we had no way to know whether the Rezniks had disclosed anything. I vividly remember the surviving younger brother crying, pounding his fist against the roof of the structure and repeating that misfortune must have befallen the family because the brothers had abandoned the young Pizman boy.

The morning after the capture of the brothers, our mood reached a new low. Shortly afterward, some survivors left Zawishcze in search of a safer location in the forests of Belin. We, however, decided that our chances for survival were much more favorable where we were. In the hope of eluding the Nazis, another group of 10 boys and two girls split from our group and built an underground shelter near a Russian partisan encampment. One member of the group was Moshke Goldberg, the brother of my future brother-in-law. All of them, with the exception of one older man, were between the ages of seventeen and twenty-one. They believed that this location would afford them protection, but they were wrong. A short time after they settled in there, one boy from that party, Moshke Aisenstat, returned to our hideout. He was pale, barely able to walk, and visibly shaken. He removed his shirt to show us two bayonet stab wounds in his chest. Moshke told us that three partisans showed up at their newly built shelter. One of them was named Mustafa, and was a crazed former soldier from the Tartar Republic (a republic in the former Soviet Union). The partisans explained to the group that they wanted them to become members of their unit. But first the Jews would have to undergo a "fitness test." They took two people outside at a time and drove a bayonet through their hearts. Then they left them dying in the snow. Those who remained inside heard screams and became alarmed. They were reassured that the men were simply being interrogated as part of the initiation.

One of the victims killed that day was Esther Lederman, the beautiful girl who had been spared by the Nazis in the lumber mill. The other girl, Tania Batalin, was only seventeen years old when she was killed. Both of these girls had brothers who were also killed during this episode. It was short of a miracle that Moshke was able to survive and recover without the slightest medical intervention. He had to be vigilant so as not to be discovered. If they realized that he remained alive, there is little doubt that they would have finished him off to eliminate all evidence. His dressings consisted of a torn undershirt, which had been washed in plain water without soap.

A Russian partisan named Sasha, whom we befriended in the forest and who belonged to the partisan unit, came to our shelter one evening and urged us to leave Zawishcze. He implied that we faced dangers beyond the danger from the Germans. He never stated his reasons, but it was obvious that he was concerned about what the partisans might do to the rest of us. Our despair and hopelessness deepened. To survive the Nazis and now face mortal peril from people who were also victims of the Nazis was almost more ironic than we could bear. We had to be on constant vigil from a German ambush and also on the lookout for anti-Semitic partisans. In essence, we were more at risk from the partisans since they knew where we were hiding. Some of the survivors heeded Sasha's advice and left for the forests of Belin. We, however, still chose to remain in Zawishcze. We felt that because of the unique relationship my family had with some of the villagers, we had a better chance of obtaining food.

After the ambush on November 1, 1942, and before my group built a new bunker, we remained with the other survivors in Zawishcze. Even in those troubled times, some of the events that transpired amused us. Easer Epelbaum, a survivor of Janów, was frightened to stay in the underground shelter and would walk all day outside the hut, hoping to be able to escape if the Germans were to suddenly overrun the camp. Fear overwhelmed him to the point that he assumed that every sound was the noise of firearms. As winter settled in, the trees froze and contracted, emitting cracking sounds that could be mistaken for shots. The noise that a woodpecker made resembled machine-gun fire as well. Easer, upon hearing those sounds, would stretch out his long arms, point with his long finger in the direction of the sounds, and in a whisper would state: *"Men shist fun dorten un dorten!"* "The shots are coming from there and there!" I also recall one night when someone passed gas in his sleep rather loudly and in rapid succession. The noise woke up another man, Moche Bezdetski, who became extremely frightened and exclaimed, "They are shooting!" He, too, was the butt of jokes for a long time to come.

Among the survivors who did not leave Zawishcze for the forest of Belin was a group of nine people — a mother and her two sons, who had escaped with me during the ambush, her husband, their niece, the poet Beryl Pomerantz, three members of the Feinstein family, and Breindel Koval. They decided to split from the main body of survivors and built a straw hut nearby as they believed it would provide them better protection. As it turned out, their efforts were in vain.

One night, in early December 1942, Nochem Krupnik from Janów and his cousin, who were members of our group, went to look for food in one of the villages. At the same time, my brother Aron, my mother, my sister Liza and I set off in the opposite direction toward the village of Chomichevo, in the hope of finding shelter in a farmer's home. The farmer, Trochim Trushko, was the brother-in-law of Radion, the man from Potapowicz who helped us after we escaped from the lumber mill. Since Shlomo Weiss was wounded and could not travel, my sister Helen remained with him. Trochim Trushko hid us that day in his hayloft. In the evening he gave us food and implored us to leave because the Nazis were in the village and he rightly feared for our safety and for the safety of his own family.

As we approached the entrance of our temporary hideout, I noticed wagon tracks. I knew that none of the survivors had a horse or wagon, so I became very suspicious. When we reached the shelter, we found out that the previous day, the Germans had attacked a nearby campsite where the previously mentioned nine Jews hid. Four of them died during that ambush. As it turned out, the two cousins who had gone in search of food were caught by the police and delivered to the Germans. The men were tortured, and one of them, Nochim Krupnik's cousin, broke down and agreed to lead the Germans to the forest. Initially he led the Nazis to an abandoned hideout. When they continued torturing him, he led them to a location where some Jews were hiding. When the Germans approached the shelter, the cousin screamed out to warn them and bolted from the wagon and was wounded. Despite the warning, the Nazis succeeded in killing the mother and her two young sons who had survived the first raid with me. The husband and father of this family was the sole survivor. To this day, I remember the empty gaze and frozen expression on that man's face after he lost his entire family. He didn't cry, but just sat there staring into space. Also among the casualties was the renowned poet, Beryl Chemerinsky. The Feinstein family was able to escape the ambush.

The campsite that was wiped out by the Germans was close to the underground hut where my sister and other survivors were staying. The cousin who betrayed the survivors managed to escape in the confusion. The death toll would have been much higher had he led the Germans to the shelter that housed the majority of the Jews. Because of his treachery, he was initially refused shelter in the underground hut, and was almost killed by the survivors. It was only after intercessions by his relative that he was allowed to remain. However, when his wounds mended, he was forced to leave the group.

In early December 1942, my brother determined that our hideout was no longer safe, so he and three other men built yet another underground shelter in a different part of the forest, in a location disclosed to no one in order to avoid any new betrayals. We were fortunate to have been raised in these woods and be so familiar with the territory. Besides Aron, the other men were a blacksmith from the nearby village of Pererub and his son, Motel. The third person, Yezik, was a young, tall, handsome, gentle boy with a fantastic sense of humor. They worked feverishly to complete the new shelter while a thaw lasted. The hideout consisted of a hole in the ground, covered with logs and dirt, and the walls were supported by logs. It had a narrow entrance and an opening for smoke to escape. There were no bathroom facilities, so people relieved themselves in the open forest. We melted the snow for cooking, but never bathed.

My family, Shlomo Weiss, Yezik, and the blacksmith and his son, moved into this new hideout on December 30, 1942. That night, as we took leave of the other survivors, we had little hope of seeing any of them again. They all envied our situation, since they were aware that our relationship with the local farmers, who remembered my father, gave us better prospects for survival. December had special significance to all of us. Hitler promised that before the end of 1942, no Jews would remain alive in occupied Europe. And yet we were still alive, with only one more day to go before the end of the year. We had sufficient food to last for a while and the snow obliterated the tracks to our hideout. For the time being, we felt safe.

For nearly six weeks, no one ventured out of the hut. We were out of touch with the world and just wondered if we were the sole surviving Jews in the forest. Eventually our food supplies dwindled and the men had to risk leaving the shelter. There was always the fear and possibility that they would be apprehended by the Nazis, tortured, and killed. The slightest delay in their return elicited unbearable anguish. When they came back from the villages, loaded with supplies, they brought news that other Jews had been seen, and we also learned that the Germans had sustained military reverses on the Russian front. After living in total squalor for such a long period of time, many of us developed scabies, a skin disease that is acquired from poor sanitary conditions and is now treated with antibiotics. Since we had no medicine, we treated ourselves with homemade remedies. Yezik helped us pass the time with wonderful jokes and tales. I especially enjoyed his mock broadcast of a soccer game.

One day we spotted a little dog near our cabin, and all of us turned ashen because we believed that the dog was leading the Germans to our hideout. We thought that surely the end had finally come. To our relief, the dog belonged to the ferryboat operator, Ochrim, who had helped us cross the river while we were fleeing from the Germans after the ghetto was liquidated. He was the only person who had the courage to venture into the woods to visit us. The encounter was highly emotional since he was the first non-Jewish acquaintance I met in the forest. Ochrim took an enormous risk to look for us. If he had stumbled upon others who didn't know him, he would likely have been killed.

In the spring of 1943, the Appelman family from Potapowicz, whom we had known before the war, joined us. Mrs. Appelman, her two sons, and her daughter escaped from Pinsk just before their ghetto was annihilated. One night, David Appelman, one of her sons, met my brother by chance while both were trying to obtain provisions. For a while the Appelmans hid near Potapowicz in an aboveground shelter, but they felt that it would be safer to move into the forest. Our underground shelter was extremely small, and to this day I have no idea how it accommodated all of us.

The spring brought fresh logistical problems. With the warmer weather, the snow began to melt and the roof and walls started to leak. Since the shelter was underground, the water rushed through the entrance and down the sides. We had no choice but to remain there and sleep above the water, on top of logs covered with hay.

When the snow melted and the ground softened, we again moved to another area of the forest. Our new shelter was more spacious and much of it was above ground. It had a window, a stove built of bricks, and walls with very expensive paneling that had been cannibalized from Graff Poslawski's castle. The door was made of mahogany, and the ceiling was high enough to enable us to walk upright. This hideout was located near the railway linking Brest Litovsk and Pinsk. The railroad was used by the Germans to supply troops and material to the Eastern Front.

Toward the end of April or early May, a band of partisans appeared in our forest and moved in with us. They had been dispatched to harass the Germans and derail the trains. I remember that one partisan was nicknamed *Lomanosof* (broken nose) because a bullet had grazed his nose. Another was a deserter from the German police force from Pilsen, Czechoslovakia. They chose to live with us since our lodging was comfortable and my mother did their laundry and prepared meals for them. In return, they brought us provisions. Often, they would have Aron and other males in our group accompany them on their military missions.

At some point, Helen developed a toothache that became progressively more severe. Eventually the swelling was so severe that it closed her eyelid. She received no dental care or painkillers, but she managed to heal. Only now, as a dentist, can I appreciate her potentially life-threatening situation. In retrospect, I also think that had it not been for her dental ailment, Helen might have been molested by the partisans. Helen's boyfriend, Shlomo Weiss, was always at risk of being shot. The partisans hinted that, by killing him, they could eliminate a rival.

The first time I was able to venture out of the underground shelter to visit other survivors was in the spring of 1943. After being cooped up in a smoky underground shelter for the whole winter, I felt enormously invigorated by the fresh air. The renewal that comes in spring held new meaning for me from then on. It does not take too much imagination to visualize how all of us looked after living in almost complete darkness for over four months. We were pale, weak, and malnourished. It was sheer joy and ecstasy to be able to get out, inhale clear air, wash, and feel soil under my feet. I believe that in May of 1943 was the first time I bathed since leaving the ghetto at the end of September of 1942. That spring, the survivors who remained in our immediate area built another shelter not too far from ours. It was a special treat to visit one another and meet some of the Jews who had arrived in the forest, since we had been separated for five months. Other Jews, who had hidden with various Gentile farmers during the winter, also joined us. There were also three men who had escaped from the Pinsk ghetto. I particularly remember a couple who emerged with a newborn baby.

In the summer of 1943, the partisan movement grew and gained strength. Their efforts to confront the Germans began to pay off, and they were able to establish secure zones in many of the surrounding villages from which they could harass the Nazis. Using only improvised explosive devices, the partisans were able to curtail train movement at night. Many who served in the German police force switched to the partisan side when the tide began to turn. These former policemen were welcomed, since they usually brought their weapons with them.

Two groups of partisans operated near us. One *otriad* (unit) was under the command of a man named Nadelin. His second-in-command was a Jew named Ilia Abramov. Nadelin was a kind and compassionate individual who took a genuine interest in the Jewish survivors and helped us enormously. Eventually Yezik — the man whose humor had entertained us in the shelter — joined Nadelin's partisan unit, left the forest of Zawishcze, and was later killed during the liberation of Czechoslovakia. One member of

Nadelin's unit was a former Russian pilot whose aircraft had been downed by the Germans. He was a very handsome young man who was constantly drunk and unpredictable. He was even accused of committing several rapes in the area. When he would approach our shelter, the girls would run and hide. At one time, he tried to assault a husky and powerful woman, Breindel Koval. Breindel wrestled the pilot to the ground and he was totally powerless against her. Her action seemed amusing, but in retrospect, those were difficult times for the females in the forest. There was a total lack of law, even though the partisans tried to develop some order and discipline within their ranks. To reinforce civility, the partisans eventually seized the pilot and executed him for his crimes. I am sure that Commander Nadelin was very happy to be rid of that scoundrel.

Another military tactic utilized by Nadelin's partisans was to confiscate provisions and cattle destined for Germany, and they were kind enough to share the booty with the Jews in the forest. The commander entrusted the care of the cows to the Jewish survivors, and we used the milk, prepared milk products, and slaughtered the cows for meat. We even set up a smokehouse and made salami. It was my responsibility, along with the other four Jewish youngsters who were in the forest, to graze the cows. By this time our nutritional intake was adequate. We enjoyed complete freedom of movement, even during daylight, and we were able to visit the surrounding villages without fear. Occasionally the Germans would venture into our area, but they would never penetrate deep into the forest. My family finally felt it was safe enough for me to spend a night in the village. I remember the strange feeling of sleeping on a bed in a farmer's house. The excitement of walking in the street and seeing people and houses was uplifting. In turn, the villagers were quite intrigued to see me as I galloped through a village on horseback; it was extremely enjoyable to spend time with our former handyman, Sakov Bogdanovicz, and his family. Before the war, his children and I had had a great deal of fun. I especially enjoyed playing in the same forests with his son, Misha, during my school vacation.

At dawn in the summer of 1943, the Germans surrounded the village of Potapowicz, burned all the homes, rounded up the inhabitants and deported them to labor camps in Germany. A Nazi collaborator, who was the alderman of the village, betrayed his own people by leading a German raiding party at nightfall across the Kanal Krulefski River. Certain that the partisans would seek retribution, the collaborator rescued his family, but refused to take along his daughter, Nastasia, from a previous marriage. Subsequently, the partisans shot her because they did not trust her. The night of the raid, my sister, Liza, was staying in the outskirts of Potapowicz, at the home of our friend Radion. We learned of the raid and were extremely concerned for her safety, but we had become experts at survival. Whenever we slept in the village, we tried to be in a house away from the center of the hamlet, near the forest. There was always an escape plan in place, so when Liza heard about the arrival of the Germans, she was able to flee safely. The inhabitants who had eluded the German dragnet settled in the forest with us.

In the spring of 1943, the Germans learned of our campsite and bombed us from the air. The planes were small, similar to a Piper Cub. The canopy of the trees was thick enough to provide adequate shelter from the air raid, but it was a most frightful experience to see the planes slowly circle above us like vultures, dropping small incendiary and cluster bombs. Fortunately, most of the ammunition exploded as soon as it hit the trees and did little damage. No injuries or fatalities resulted, but the raids lasted three days. Since the Germans now knew our location, we decided to move once again. This time, all the survivors in the forest of Zawishcze elected to build their lodgings in the same area, and we formed a small community.

That summer, a poisonous snake bit Liza and she almost died. Obviously there was no anti-venom serum, and her leg swelled up. Consequently she developed a high fever. In desperation, she was taken to a faith healer and luckily she recovered without any ill effects. That summer we also learned that there had been an uprising in the Warsaw Ghetto. The news came as a complete surprise to us, since we believed that all Polish Jews had been killed. That fall and winter we learned that Germany was losing the war and so our resolve to survive increased. One day, the Germans bombed a partisan group in our vicinity with heavy payloads. The ground shook around us, our lodgings were damaged from the vibration, and the sand that camouflaged our underground shelter poured inside. We were fortunate that this air raid was not directed at our hideout. But we also realized that the risk of such raids was rising as the Germans retreated and pulled their planes out of previously occupied Russian territory. They were likely to use the aircraft to bomb every suspicious site in the forest.

CHAPTER 12

The Retreat to Rafalofka

Early in 1944, the German army began its retreat on the Eastern Front. At that point, the number of German soldiers in our region increased. The air raids were more frequent and the payloads heavier. We were even shelled by artillery. Although the partisan movement was better organized and Russian planes began to parachute arms to them, they were no match for the German forces in open combat. We realized that the Germans could not be kept out of the forest much longer. At that time we had no idea when the Russians would liberate our area. We were also aware that the partisans contemplated abandoning the forest, so we waited for a signal from them.

One evening, a Jewish partisan, Avremel Feinstein, informed us that his unit was going to evacuate the area. We piled our meager belongings and provisions onto a horse-drawn wagon and set off on a journey without knowing our destination's end. We had to cross a large stretch of land that was still under German occupation. There was only enough room in the wagon for my mother, Mrs. Appelman, and Shlomo Weiss, who had contracted typhus. The rest of us walked the entire way. The hunger and fatigue made me fall asleep as I traveled on foot, and I often found myself veering off the road. We could not take turns riding on the wagon since the two women and Shlomo were unable to walk. I wanted to balance myself by holding onto the wagon, but this would have placed an extra burden on the animal.

The territory we had to cross was inhabited by nationalistic Ukrainians who were Nazi sympathizers. They hated Jews and Poles, were opposed to the Soviet regime, and anticipated retribution from the Russian authorities because of their collaboration with the Nazis. In the face of the advancing Russian forces, they hid and formed renegade bands. These Ukrainian villagers lived in semi-isolation and were probably the poorest people in all of Poland. Their passionate hatred for Poles and Jews dated back to Taras Bulba, a Ukrainian nationalist commander of a Cossack regiment that was responsible for many pogroms under the czar's regime. We felt defenseless traveling through this territory. As we moved along, our convoy was swelled with the arrival of Jews and non-Jews alike who were abandoning the forests. Along the way, we met some survivors from Janów, who had been hiding in the Belin forest and whom we hadn't seen since we left the ghetto.

We crossed that stretch of land in early spring while some of the streams were still covered with ice. Midway through our journey, the sun became warmer, the ice melted, and we had to cross open streams. At one crossing, we all piled into the wagon in the hope that the horse would pull us across without getting stuck in the water. However, in mid-stream the horse stopped, and Liza and I jumped into the river to help pull the wagon out. We then continued walking the rest of the way. As the sun set, it became very cold and our clothing froze on us, making it difficult to walk.

Finding a place to rest during the long march was always a formidable task. The sheer number of the evacuees overwhelmed the capacity of the villages. Finding food was an even greater undertaking, since we didn't have valuables to barter. On the third night of our journey, we arrived at a village. After much searching, we were able to secure lodging for the night with a farmer. The small house could barely accommodate our party, so I decided to sleep outside in the wagon. Shortly after I fell asleep, Aron woke me and told me that we had to leave the house, since Shlomo, who was severely ill with a fever, said that he overheard a conversation in which the farmer said he was plotting to kill us. He went so far as to insist that the conversation took place in Hebrew. We suspected that Shlomo was hallucinating and that the conversation probably had not transpired, but we did not want to take any chances, so we all left the house and spent the remainder of the night outdoors. The farmer seemed somewhat perplexed.

I have alluded several times to the generosity and benevolence of my father. The next anecdote further illustrates my point. One night during our retreat from the forest, we lodged in another farmer's home. He made derogatory remarks about Jews in general, but recalled that before the war he had worked for a Jew, and proceeded to extol that man's virtues. He said that the man was the only good Jew he had ever known. From his description of the work he did and the location of his job, we realized that he was talking about our father. Though we tried to tell him that the person he lauded was our father, he refused to believe us.

During the retreat, all able men were ordered to join a partisan fighting unit. Aron and the other men above the age of eighteen departed, leaving the women, children, and disabled behind to fend for themselves. However, shortly after the men left, Aron and the others returned to our convoy. There was no central authority or central command, and no one knew what was going on. One illustration of the general lack of law and order came when Ukrainian nationals killed and mutilated a man named Shepsel. He was a survivor from our town who had become a partisan. This news was both sad and frightful.

One day, as our column of refugees trudged along, we spotted a German plane. To word this more accurately, the German pilot spotted us. The plane circled overhead, but then flew off without firing a shot. To this day, I have no idea why the pilot did not fire upon us. Perhaps he had already had his fill of bloodshed or simply was an honorable man who knew that we were not a military convoy. Had he decided to strafe us, enormous casualties would have resulted.

Toward the end of our journey, everyone was exhausted and many became ill. One of the casualties was the little baby girl who had been born to the couple in hiding. I remember how the mother lamented that her child was dying, but no one could help the infant. The baby was breathing very rapidly, barely making audible sounds, and the mother tearfully sobbed to her husband, "Yosel, the baby is dying." Soon, the baby girl did expire, and she was buried in a field.

In early April 1944, we crossed the Stir River near the town of Rafalofka. It was here that we encountered Russian soldiers for the first time. We were all relieved and thought that our travails were over, but our happiness was short-lived. Once again, we were on our own and forced to fend for ourselves. I hoped that once I left German occupation, I would receive preferential treatment because I was a survivor. My dream soon vanished. Within days after our arrival, my brother and the other surviving men were drafted into the Russian army. As my brother was placed on the train to boot camp, I stood at the station, fearing that I would never see him again. My brother tried to comfort me and urged me to be courageous; nevertheless, I could not be consoled. There I stood, all alone on the platform, and as the train pulled out, tears streamed down my cheeks. I remained forlorn and waited on the platform until the train was completely out of sight. My protector was no longer there to take care of me. It was heartbreaking to think that Aron, having survived the massacres, would possibly die with victory almost within reach.

In the Ukraine, the government did not issue food and we had no means to buy or barter. Food was extremely scarce and hunger pervaded Rafalofka. I noticed that some people were cooking meat on an outdoor fire in the compound where we initially lived. When no one was looking, I grabbed a bone with meat from the cauldron, and gobbled it up. Nothing that I have eaten since that day has tasted as good.

Because the Russian front was situated not far from Rafalofka, many soldiers were stationed in the area, so Mother would often wash or mend army uniforms and receive food for her services. There was also a potato storage area nearby. The Russian army dug up most of the yield, but we were allowed to scavenge for leftovers. To do this, we dug through the dirt by hand and occasionally would find a frozen potato. Our inadequate diet and poor hygiene made us susceptible to disease. Shlomo Weiss became critically ill as soon as we reached Rafalofka. Initially, he was admitted to a local hospital, but the army then transferred him to a hospital in Sarno, a town approximately twenty miles away. Sarno was located at an important railway junction, and the Germans bombed the town nightly. We are not sure if he died in one of the air raids or succumbed to his disease, but we never saw or heard from him again.

The next victim to be stricken with typhus was my sister, Helen. When she became ill, though, the rest of us were able to provide her with nourishment. I recall going from house to house in Rafalofka, begging the local people for a cup of milk for her. Unfortunately, my mother, Liza, and I, also caught the disease in rapid succession. The hospital was staffed by overworked nurses and by a *feldcher*, the equivalent of a nurse practitioner. There was no medication available, not even an aspirin. For much of the time I was delirious, and therefore, I cannot fully recall the extent of my illness. Slowly we all recovered, but the effects of the disease lingered for some time, especially because we lacked proper nutrition and we were all emaciated. The women were affected the most. Their hair was completely shorn to facilitate hygiene, and it took a long time for it to grow back.

When the Red Army launched its spring offensive in May 1944, the soldiers stationed in Rafalofka moved out and we were left in dangerous circumstances. First, our source of sustenance dried up and then the area was left unprotected. Anti-Soviet renegade bands soon infiltrated the region. One night, rumors spread of an impending attack from those bandits. I am not sure whether the rumor was accurate, but all the Jews abandoned their dwellings and spent the night in the open field. This was the ideal set-up for an ambush, since we were gathered like unprotected sheep ready for the slaughter. Once again, we felt helpless and had no idea where to turn. Fortunately nothing happened. The authorities must have realized that they had to prevent the towns from being taken over by the thugs, for shortly after that incident, Russian soldiers were deployed in Rafalofka.

While in the forest, I learned to make moonshine vodka, and put this expertise to good use upon our arrival in Rafalofka. We could obtain all our basic necessities by bartering vodka. To supplement our earnings my mother baked rolls and I sold as much as I could to the Russian soldiers at the railroad station. Eventually, my sisters were able to get clerical jobs at a governmental office, while I attended school. This was the first time I enjoyed school, and I did well.

In the summer of 1944, I saw transports of German prisoners of war passing through town. They were on their way, I presume, to Siberia. This was my first face-to-face encounter with Germans since I escaped from the ghetto. Though they were locked inside the freight cars, the Germans still intimidated me and I did not dare reveal my Jewish identity.

The Soviets staged their offensive on the Belarus front in the early spring of that year, and drove the Germans out of the rest of occupied Russia. For weeks we listened intently to daily radio broadcasts and followed the progress of the war. During each broadcast, the newscaster read the names of the cities and towns that had been liberated from the Nazis, and we hoped to eventually hear the name of our hometown, Janów. The names of the places were familiar to us — Slonim, Baranovitch and, finally, Pinsk. We then began to plan our departure for the city of Pinsk, in order to be closer to Janów. Since both my sisters had found work, they had to get permission to quit their jobs. Unfortunately, working for the Russian system was tantamount to being an indentured servant. A person who left a job without permission was treated like a deserter. Helen was able to obtain her release by putting in extra time during the evening and weekends, but Liza's employer was not as generous. Because of this, we had to escape from Rafalofka without anyone discovering our plan. On our journey home, Mrs. Appelman, her 25-year-old daughter and her 6-year-old son joined us.

CHAPTER 13

The Journey to Pinsk

We hoped to arrive in Pinsk within two days. However, the trip turned out to be an odyssey. Initially, we took the train to Sarno, which was at a railroad junction. We hoped to catch a connecting train to Pinsk from there, a distance of less than 100 miles. We were not aware that the railroad tracks and bridges between the two cities had been destroyed by the retreating Germans, and that the trip could only be made by foot or by horse and carriage. These options were not viable, since we feared that former German collaborators had the territory under their control. We couldn't and didn't want to go back to Rafalofka. We were then informed that train connections to Pinsk were possible only from the city of Brest Litovsk. In order to reach Brest Litovsk, we would have to exit the Soviet Union at the border crossing in Chelm, continue to Lublin, Poland, and then re-enter Russia at Brest Litovsk — a detour of 500 miles! This trip is analogous to someone traveling from New York City to Philadelphia by first traveling to Canada, and then continuing down to Philadelphia. Still, we had no other option and decided to take the risk, preposterous as it was. I had never heard of anyone who had been able to escape Russia. Yet here we were, leaving the Soviet Union illegally and re-entering it without visas or travel permits.

I was shocked at the devastation in Sarno. The railway station and surrounding area were a sea of twisted steel and rubble. People still lived amid the wreckage, and the railway center functioned despite the enormous destruction. We found a freight train that was transporting tanks to the battlefront. Helen was able to bribe a Russian soldier to hide us under the tanks on the troop transport. The train made a stopover in Rafalofka, which made us uneasy, for we feared being arrested because of Liza's unauthorized departure from her job. The train then took us as far as the city of Kovel, where we spent a day or two until we were able to find an army transport headed for Lublin, Poland. Again, for a price, we were hidden in the equipment transport. After reaching Lublin, we remained at the train station until we discovered a transport returning to Russia via Brest Litovsk.

While in Lublin, we learned for the first time about Hitler's death factories and of the extermination camp called Maidanek. Some of the soldiers went to see this death camp and described the horrors they witnessed. At the time, the soldiers' stories made little impact on me since I couldn't comprehend the inhuman methods of killing.

Food was extremely scarce on the train, and we had to drink contaminated water from open pipes. I contracted amebic dysentery and suffered tremendously, and since the train had no toilet facilities, I had to hold everything in until the train came to a stop. We finally arrived in Brest Litovsk, the crossing point between Poland and Russia, and were promptly arrested and detained by the border guards. We proceeded to relate our entire story to them.

The interrogator could not understand how we had gotten as far as we did, and we couldn't fault him, since the whole story sounded extremely incredible. Our papers were confiscated and we were ordered not to leave the bombed-out railway station. Nevertheless, Helen went to tour the city and met one of the arresting officers in the street. He told her that walking around the city without any identification papers was extremely dangerous and urged her to return to the station. He indicated that she could be jailed and would vanish without a trace.

We were held in Brest Litovsk for two days and then, mysteriously, were allowed to leave. In Brest Litovsk we met some non-Jewish young men from Janów who had been drafted into the Russian army. The look on their faces when they gazed upon us is impossible to describe. They probably thought we were ghosts. We learned from them that Janów had been completely destroyed by the retreating German army. After 10 arduous days, we finally boarded the train that would take us to Pinsk. Along the way, it made a brief stop in Janów. The railroad station was right across from the lumber mill that had been our initial point of departure after the ghetto was annihilated. Although the stopover was short, it evoked many memories, some nostalgic, but most of them sad and extremely painful.

For obvious reasons, we had no intention of remaining in Janów. The town had been completely destroyed, our loved ones had been killed, and no Jews remained. Living with the ghosts of the past was more than we could bear. It would take me seven months to gain the courage to return to Janów, even though it was just 20 miles way from Pinsk. I saw the rubble of the ghetto and walked the streets of the town that had once been a vibrant Jewish community. For a very long time, I was unable to discuss or talk about the events that transpired there. Indeed, I did not broach or reflect on the subject until fifty years had elapsed. I have since learned that the remains of all the Jewish victims were exhumed and burned by the Nazis before they abandoned my town, to conceal their crimes. Only ashes remained of both the ghetto and its inhabitants.

CHAPTER 14

Pinsk At Last

Our arrival in Pinsk marked the beginning of our return to "normalcy." The military front was west of us, near Warsaw, and we no longer feared air raids or other attacks. But as we had no place to turn, we just stayed at the bombed-out railroad station, while Helen, who had attended school in Pinsk prior to the war, went to scout the town. The city was severely damaged, living quarters were at a premium, and we had no money or valuables. Helen was able to locate a survivor, Benjamin Wolf, who invited us to stay with him, since he believed that we had something to offer him. He had the false notion that because we came from Poland we must have brought some valuable items. I recall spending Yom Kippur in his house. When it came time to break the fast, we had little to eat, while he gorged himself on apples dipped in honey, a traditional treat to signal a sweet year. I still shudder remembering his lack of sensitivity. All of Mr. Wolf's actions were motivated by profit, and when he realized that there was no advantage in keeping us at his home, he asked us to leave.

Fortunately, Helen soon met a Jewish young man, Grisha Shepetinsky, a survivor who had fought with the partisans, and was now a Russian policeman. Grisha was a total stranger, yet he was willing to provide us with a roof over our heads and share his scant rations. At first, our relationship was very formal, but as time went by, we grew very close. I believe that, with us, he rediscovered a new family. (Before the war, he had lived with his parents and sister in the city of Slonim.) Grisha often came home intoxicated with his characteristic smile of guilt. My mother would often admonish him with the words, "What would your mother say if she saw you in this state?" She urged him to change his behavior. In the end she actually succeeded. When we decided to leave Russia, we persuaded him to join us. He eventually settled in Israel and changed his name to Zvi Shefet. We have remained close friends to this day. My siblings and I regard Zvi and his wife, Gita, and their kin, to be part of our extended family.

Early in 1945, Aron Karolinski, who hid with us in the Janów lumberyard after the ghetto was annihilated, also came to live with us in Pinsk. He was a very enterprising young man with an overwhelming drive to survive. He, too, was drafted into the army. The only way a Russian soldier could avoid fighting on the front was either to be killed or become disabled. At first, Karolinski extracted his own teeth in the hope that this disfigurement would keep him away from the front. Eventually he even mutilated himself by putting a bullet through his right hand. Even the slightest suspicion of such an offense usually resulted in court-martial and execution or, at best, deportation to a penal squad, resulting in the most dangerous assignment at the front. However, he was able to bribe some officials and was shipped to a hospital in Pinsk. When he lived in the Janów ghetto, Mr. Karolinski had stashed away a large sum of gold coins near his house. He was able to recover this treasure and use it to bribe the army doctors to certify him as a disabled veteran, and thus, was never sent back to the battlefield.

The rations were inadequate in Pinsk, and we certainly could not afford to buy food on the black market. Thankfully, Mr. Karolinski was able to barter and obtain scarce provisions. He always shared them with the rest of us. He was extremely generous and helpful to my family while we lived in Pinsk, and he was a vital asset to us. We finally had nutritious meals, after barely eating anything for such an extended period of time.

As soon as we were settled in Pinsk, I enrolled in a school. There I met some other Jewish children who had survived. Most of these youngsters had come from the village of Sernik, a small town not far from Pinsk, located in the Pripet Marshes. The rest of the school population was made up of local youth, or children of Communist Party officials who had resettled in Pinsk. I felt very much out of place at first, since I was poorly clothed and rather emaciated after my bout with amebic dysentery. One day on my way home from school I overheard two girls making fun of me. As one can imagine, I was humiliated by their remarks. After I established myself in the United States, I fantasized about going back to Pinsk and confronting the girls just to prove how much I had accomplished.

On visits to Janów, we checked with the local post office to learn, if, by chance, we had any mail. On one of these visits, the postman gave Helen a postcard from an Esther Shoroshevsky, who had immigrated from Janów to America before the war. The postcard, which was addressed to Esther's parents and siblings, inquired about whether any of her family members had survived the mass murder. Helen wrote back and informed Esther that her entire family had perished. She also told Esther about the status of our family, and asked her to search for my mother's sister, Sarah Greenberg, who lived in Brooklyn. Mrs. Shoroshevsky immediately got in touch with my aunt, who contacted my mother's two other sisters living in the United States. However, my relatives were unable to contact us, since we were constantly on the move.

After my brother Aron was drafted, we received letters from him regularly. We prayed and hoped for the best, but in view of the enormous number of casualties the Russian army was sustaining, we always anticipated the worst.

Receiving mail was a small consolation, since it proved only that my brother had been alive before the letter had been mailed. We knew that he was with the First Ukrainian Front, so we closely followed their progress. At one point the letters from Aron stopped abruptly. We concluded that he was a casualty of war, and prepared ourselves for the worst. I had the horrible feeling as though I had lost my father again. My mother was despondent. It was very difficult to contemplate losing Aron after having survived such a prolonged ordeal. We never forgot his devotion to and sacrifice for his family. But then after a hiatus of three or four weeks, a nurse who was caring for my brother informed us that he was alive, that he had been severely wounded and was hospitalized in the city of Gorky. We were unaware of the extent of his injuries, so we greeted this news with mixed emotions. We prayed for what seemed impossible — that his wounds were severe enough to keep him from returning to the battlefield, but not serious enough to threaten his life.

Our first impulse was that one of us should visit Aron in Gorky. The logical person to make the trip was Helen, since she was now the eldest and had some experience traveling. Helen had worked as a civilian bookkeeper for the Russian army, and she often used the train for official business. Army personnel received preferential passage, so Helen bought an army dress on the black market and put it on to look like a soldier. She also illegally appropriated a travel permit from the unit she worked for, since each passenger had to obtain a document stating the origin and destination of his or her voyage. Grisha Shepetinsky filled out the document, stating that Helen was traveling to Gorky on a military mission. She took along some clothing in the hope that she might be able to bribe the hospital administrator and obtain my brother's release.

Her journey was filled with risks. The train schedule was erratic, the stations bombed out, and food or lodging unavailable along the way. And although Helen wore an army uniform, her topcoat distinguished her as civilian. If she was caught in this masquerade, she could be executed. Nevertheless, she boarded the train in Pinsk and arrived at a junction where she hoped to catch a connecting train to Moscow. Unfortunately, she missed the connection, and the next train was not scheduled until the following day.

Helen waited at the station with no place to go. She was soon approached by two soldiers. They told her that they knew of a place to stay and invited her to join them. Helen agreed. That evening the soldiers made derogatory comments about Jews, berating the Jews' lack of patriotism and involvement on the front. Helen became very upset and could not contain herself, and she began to cry. She informed the soldiers that she was Jewish, and admonished them by pointing out that her brother Aron was a soldier who was gravely wounded. The soldiers then behaved like perfect gentleman the entire night, and it never occurred to Helen at that time that she might be molested. Helen and the two soldiers arrived at the station the next day and boarded the train to Moscow. During the trip an inspector checked her document and found a discrepancy. He became suspicious when he saw her wearing the civilian coat, and asked her to come along with him. The two soldiers who were in the compartment with her came to her aid and stated to the inspector, "If you like this girl, just come out and say it outright." The inspector was embarrassed, so he relented and returned her documents. Throughout the trip, Helen was extremely concerned that the package she was carrying with her might be stolen or lost.

Helen finally arrived in Moscow, where she needed to change trains for Gorky. That meant leaving the main terminal and taking a subway to another station, which required going through a checkpoint and yet another document inspection. There were two exit lines at the gate, one for civilians and the other for military personnel. She decided to take the exit reserved for military personnel. Helen's documents were confiscated, and she was asked to stand aside and wait. Helen argued that she was not familiar with Moscow, and that she was traveling with two soldiers who were supposed to tell her where to go. Fortunately, her documents were returned to her and she proceeded to the station where she could find the train to Gorky. One of the most frightening aspects of her trip, according to Helen, was when she had to use an escalator. Since she had never seen one before, she panicked and stood frozen. Finally, a man took her by the arm and helped her get on. That terrifying experience, to this day, makes her ill at ease every time she has to climb onto an escalator.

There were no seats available on the train to Gorky. Helen realized that there was a supervisor for each compartment checking documents and tickets, and that each seat number was assigned and written on the traveler's document. At this point Helen feared for her life. She spotted a car where soldiers were pushing themselves onto the train. She took a chance and rushed into the car along with them. A female inspector saw Helen's black coat and screamed out, "You can't go in there!" The inspector then began to search for her in the car, while screaming that a civilian got on the train. Helen had the sense to take her coat off, and since she had her army uniform under it, was able to blend in with the crowd.

At last, Helen arrived in Gorky and inquired about getting to the hospital. She was told to take a certain bus. Lacking any experience in a big city, she tried to get on the first bus she saw, when luckily a man overheard her and informed her that she was on the wrong bus. He then gave her the correct directions. Aron was taken completely by surprise when he saw Helen. He had been severely wounded in the stomach by artillery shrapnel and was recovering after surgery and ready to be discharged from the army. Gorky lacked accommodations, but Helen was able to secure a place for herself and stayed with one of the nurses. When Aron was well enough to be discharged, the hospital administration issued my sister new documents stating that she was accompanying a wounded veteran back home. This time she was legally assigned to a seat on the train and the trip home was completely uneventful.

Helen's journey might seem like it was an exciting adventure, but it was fraught with danger. My sister was barely twenty years old at that time. She was a small-town girl lacking worldly sophistication, had never been to a large city, and was extremely naïve. Yet she was willing to risk her own welfare to help her brother. At no time did she express any reservation or reluctance about her mission. Helen's trip was a perilous exploration into the unknown and she truly deserves the biblical description "*Eyshet Chail*," a woman of valor (Psalm 31).

When Aron saw me last, I was still small for my age. Now, 12 months later, I had grown and looked like a teenager. When I greeted him, Aron did not recognize me, and he asked my sisters who I was.

In Pinsk, the local Soviet militia conducted frequent house-to-house searches for army deserters, especially at night. One day, two Jewish deserters came to our house and asked for lodging. Our house was always open to strangers in need, and naturally we let them in. Although we had only three rooms, at times there were as many as fifteen people sleeping there. On the evening in which the deserters arrived, Grisha came home and informed us that the police were searching the homes in the area. We were all frightened, but were not about to betray these men. Grisha stood outside our house in his uniform all night, and when his fellow police officers from the precinct came to search our home, he told them that he lived there, so they left.

In April 1945, the local authorities posted a map of Europe in the center of town, depicting the military progress of the Allies in Germany. I could see the circle closing in around Berlin. Around that time, I witnessed the hanging of a man in Pinsk who had been a Nazi collaborator and an anti-Soviet guerrilla. Gallows were erected one morning, and a crowd gathered in the town square as if for a festive occasion. The truck carrying the prisoner drove up to the gallows and an officer announced the prisoner's crimes. He pronounced the verdict: "Death by hanging to the traitor!" The crowd applauded and shouted with approval. As they placed the noose around the prisoner's neck, he fought and moved his head around, trying to escape. I remember how at that moment I made a motion with my hands as if to assist the soldiers in their task. I left the scene of the hanging with a feeling of revenge, fulfillment, and personal satisfaction. Since the corpse was left in the square for a full day, I made more than one trip to view it.

Each important radio broadcast from Moscow began with the music of *"Shyroka Strana Moya Rodnaya"* (the same song the Ukrainian collaborator had whistled in the lumber mill as he was hunting for Jews). On May 8, 1945, at about midnight, I awoke to that tune and realized that we were about to hear an important announcement. And so it was. The broadcast proclaimed Germany's surrender. By then, I was almost 15 years old.

CHAPTER 15

Farewell to Russia, On to Berlin

As World War II drew to an end, we longed to leave Russia, but the borders were sealed. However, an opportunity presented itself in June of 1945. At the end of the war, Poland and the Soviet Union signed an accord allowing ethnic Poles and Jews who had been Polish nationals prior to September 1, 1939, to leave Russia. This was the break we had waited for and we registered to obtain our permits. We also urged our friend Grisha Shepetinsky to join us. For Grisha, obtaining the proper documents was a difficult task since he was a policeman who possessed state secrets and was also a member of the Comsomol, a Communist organization one level below full Communist Party membership. He took a great risk by trying to get out. If he had been refused the exit permit, he would have fallen into disgrace and been dismissed from the police department. When he presented his request, his commander sarcastically said, "What do you mean you want to go to Poland? Maybe I would like to go to America? This is nonsense." Nevertheless, Grisha did obtain permission and was able to join us on our way to Poland.

By August, our family was on the move once again. We loaded what little we had into a boxcar and, with many other émigrés, prepared to depart. Our destination was Lodz, Poland. We persuaded Getzel Shuster, a teenage survivor, to join us. (He was the youngster who had wrenched himself out of an anti-Semitic woman's grip as she tried to deliver him to the Germans when he escaped the march to the execution pits.) Since his decision to leave was a last-minute thought, he didn't have the proper documents. We hid him under mounds of hay in the cattle car and he was not detected at the border. On our way to Lodz, I saw long transports of sealed boxcars holding German prisoners of war. They looked not unlike their Jewish victims as they were transported east to Russian labor camps. As soon as we crossed into Poland, we heard the Polish nationals raise their ugly voices, denouncing the Jews on the train. No matter where we went, no matter what we had been through, we could not escape this pulsing hatred. The Polish authorities never guaranteed our safety, and we frequently heard stories of Jews being killed by Poles.

In Lodz, survivors registered their names in a permanent record book. Unfortunately, we found none of our relatives or friends in the register. We also came in contact with many concentration camp survivors. It was then that the full extent of the horrors became evident to us. Despite what we had already witnessed, the survivors' stories seemed too gruesome to believe. We remained in Lodz for just three months. Aron Karolinski, who left Russia before us, repaid our hospitality for taking him into our home in Pinsk, by inviting us to stay in his apartment until we figured out our next move. We were aware that there was an underground railroad, under the auspices of the Palestinian Jewish Agency, organized to smuggle Jews out of Poland via Czechoslovakia or Germany.

Our initial destination was the American Occupation Zone in Germany. The section of Germany occupied by the Russians was designated as East Germany, while the territories occupied by the Americans, British and French were designated as West Germany. When we left Lodz in early December 1945, we had no idea where we would wind up in the American zone, but we decided to take the risk crossing the border. The Jewish owner of the safe house in Stetin knew some Russian army truck drivers who regularly traveled to East Berlin. For a fee, he agreed to arrange our escape. It made me feel ill knowing that he was profiting from our misery. The following day, my family, along with other survivors, was loaded onto a truck headed for Berlin. We were detained at the border between Poland and East Germany, and the thought of being caught at this stage was deeply discouraging.

Fortunately, the Polish border patrols had no authority to inspect Russian cargo and we were able to cross the border without incident. After being bounced around in the back of a cold truck for two hours, we arrived at an assembly place — a former synagogue on Ricker Strasse, in East Berlin. Members of a Jewish agency met us and provided food and shelter. They also arranged our transfer to the American Occupation Zone. We remained in East Berlin for approximately 10 days. To my delight, Berlin was completely devastated. It gave me enormous satisfaction to walk freely in the capital of the Third Reich.

From Berlin we were taken in American army trucks to Hanover in the British Occupation Zone. From there we traveled to Frankfurt and eventually wound up in a displaced persons camp in Lampertheim, near Manheim, which was located in the American Occupation Zone.

After almost four years of living in the camp, my family was given the opportunity to immigrate to the United States. We were able to show that we had relatives in Connecticut who would sponsor us, and therefore, we would not be a burden on the welfare system. Mother and Helen departed first. Then, on May 10, 1949, after 10 days at sea, I reached the shores of New York City and saw the Statue of Liberty. Liza and Aron were the last to arrive, and soon joined us in Hartford, Connecticut. I finally experienced true freedom, and this young Jewish survivor was given the opportunity to begin life anew.

About the Author

Lewis Reznik, a retired dentist living in Westchester County, New York, speaks to school and community groups about the lessons of the Holocaust and tutors students preparing for their Bar Mitzvah. Dr. Reznik was born in Janów Polaski, Poland. When World War II began, he was 9 years old. After Germany invaded its neighbors, Nazi killing squads swept cities, towns and the countryside, seeking and slaughtering Jews, including his father, sister, grandmother and many other relatives. He and his family faced wrenching horrors and challenges, first in a ghetto created by the Nazis and then living off the land for nearly two years after fleeing to the surrounding forests with others who escaped death. In 1944, Russian troops liberated Poland. Lewis spent nearly four years in a displaced persons camp in the American Occupation Zone near Frankfurt, Germany. He moved to the United States in 1949 at the age of 19 and settled in Hartford, Connecticut, where he attended night school and obtained his high school diploma at 23. He received degrees from the University of Connecticut,

Long Island University and the Columbia University School of Dental and Oral Surgery. He and his wife, Louise, raised two daughters, one of whom inspired him to dig into his memories and write this book.

This is Dr. Reznik's explanation for writing *A Boy's Holocaust*: "I want to share my experiences in order to inform and educate others about the cruelty perpetrated by the Nazis and their collaborators, and contrast that with the compassion and love on the part of those who risked their lives to help preserve mine. Also, I provide living proof that the Holocaust did occur despite those who continue to deny it."